Extraordinary People in
Extraordinary Times

Extraordinary People in Extraordinary Times

Heroes, Sheroes, and Villains

Patrick M. Mendoza

1999
Libraries Unlimited
Teacher Ideas Press
A Division of Greenwood Publishing Group
Englewood, Colorado

Libraries Unlimited
Teacher Ideas Press
A Division of Greenwood Publishing Group
P.O. Box 6633
Englewood, CO 80155-6633
1-800-237-6124
www.lu.com/tip

Library of Congress Cataloging-in-Publication Data

Mendoza, Patrick M.
    Extraordinary people in extraordinary times : heroes, sheroes, and villains / Patrick M. Mendoza.
    x, 142 p. 17x25 cm.
    Includes index.
    ISBN 1-56308-611-5 (pbk.)
    1. Heroes--United States Biography. 2. Women heroes--United States Biography. 3. United States--Biography. I. Title.
CT214.M46 1999
920.073--dc21
  [B]
                                        99-14238
                                           CIP

To my wife Dona
and in memory of my friend Stanley "Smokey" Sorenson

Contents

Preface   ix

Acknowledgments   x

1   Mochi   1

2   The Shadow on the Wall   9

3   The Medal and the Lady: The Mary Edwards Walker Story   15

   Ten Interesting Facts about the Congressional Medal of Honor   19

4   Nathan's Legacy   22

   Dempsey Shorts   25

5   Mother Maggard   26

6   Silas Soule: A Forgotten Hero of Sand Creek   28

7   Theodosia: A Lady Lost   39

8   Jules Bledsoe: The Voice   44

9   Charles Gates Dawes: He Won the Nobel Peace Prize and Wrote a Song That Went to the Top 40   46

   Ten Interesting Facts about Presidents and Vice-Presidents   49

10   The Day Doris Miller Became a Man   53

   The First Shots Fired on December 7, 1941   55

11   Billie and Patches   56

12   Sam Antonio: The Last Acoma to Survive   59

13   Shoichi Yokoi: The Last Japanese Soldier   71

        The Last Officer to Surrender   73

14   One Extraordinary Event: The Day They Hanged
        an Elephant   74

        The Hartleypoole Chimp Incident   77

15   Governor Ralph Carr: A Man of Compassion   78

        Interesting Facts about the Internment Camps   83

16   Jeannette Pickering Rankin: The Lady from Montana   85

        Quotes from Jeannette Pickering Rankin   92

17   Villains: Lavinia Fisher   93

        Footnotes in Crime   96

18   Those Weren't Ladies, They Were Pirates: Anne
        Bonny and Mary Read   97

        Pirate Briefs   100

19   Jonita   102

20   Jóse Marti: His Eloquence Is Still Heard   111

        Quotes from Jóse Marti   120

21   Daisy Anderson: "I Just Want People to Get Along
        with Each Other"   122

22   Doctor Victor Westphall and Angel Fire   126

References   132

Index   140

Preface

Many of the stories in this book started as oral tales. I first heard the story about the pirate Blackbeard being killed in North Carolina on Cape Hatteras Island in 1966. While I was in the Navy, stationed in Norfolk, a Virginia friend of mine and I took a weekend "liberty" to camp out on the then nearly deserted island. While there we met an elderly "Outer Banker," as the inhabitants were called. My friend and I were held spellbound for a couple of hours as this eighty-two-year-old man told us incredible tales, not only about Blackbeard, but about Theodosia Alston and those two "fool yankee boys" who had come to the island with their "fandangled contraption that brought all them other yankees there for days." He was talking about Wilbur and Orville Wright. He had witnessed the first flight of man.

I have never forgotten those stories or that man, although his name is lost to me. From that time on I have cherished the "forgotten" heroes and villains and events in history that I have run across.

Someone new to the world of storytelling once asked me whom I studied under. I started laughing, because in those days there weren't really what you'd call "professional storytellers"; there were about a dozen of us who didn't know about each other. My answer to the question was "the hundreds of people I've met and talked to all these years."

Since I began my career in storytelling and music some twenty-three years ago, many of those people have passed on, but I still have their memories and those incredible tales of heroes, sheroes, and villains. I have finally pulled together twenty-two of these tales on paper, although I have enough stories like these to fill another couple of volumes. Until I do, enjoy this collection.

Patrick Mendoza
December 1998
Denver, Colorado

Acknowledgments

I wish to thank the following people for their help through the stories they shared with me. Teddi Duncan, a wonderful Acoma storyteller, for introducing me to her uncle Sam Antonio. Sam Antonio, who has treated me like family since my first visit with him four years ago. Renee Boveé, of the Wyoming State Arts Council, who invited me to her home one night to share the incredible story of her mother Jonita Bonham through her letters home and military records. I would also like to thank Phill Sill, wherever he may be, for telling me the first version of "Shadow on the Wall" way back in 1977. And the late Sarah Walker and her family, for so many other pieces of information about Rutherford County, North Carolina. Many thanks to Henry Lowenstein and Bob Carr for the incredible life story of Governor Ralph Carr. And to Archie Willis, my long-time friend, for many of the Charleston tales and to the late Clark Wilcox, who allowed me to videotape our conversations about the low country of South Carolina. I would also like to thank my Cheyenne family, Terry, Bertha, Everette, and John, for the story of Mochi. And the good folks of the South Carolina Historic Society, the State Archives of North Carolina, the Colorado Historic Society, and the Denver Public Library Western History Department. Last, but not least, thanks to Dr. Victor Westphall, my friend and mentor, and my brother-in-arms Michael Peterson; we've done some healing together. To those I have forgotten, forgive me. It was due to a "senior moment."

Mochi

On November 29, 1864, in southeastern Colorado, Colonel John Milton Chivington charged down on a peaceful village of Cheyenne who were camped on a dry river bed named Big Sandy Creek. This incident, known as the Sand Creek Massacre, has been written and debated about ever since, but the story has not been told through the voices of the Cheyenne who survived that terrible day. One of those survivors was a woman called Mochi.

According to the old ones who knew her story, Mochi was one of the fiercest of all Cheyenne warriors. She belonged to the Bow Stringer Society, and along with her second husband, Medicine Water, was among the last of the Southern Cheyenne to surrender to the United States Army in 1875. She was the only Native American woman in American history who has ever been sent to prison as a prisoner of war. And the story of her transformation from woman to warrior began as have so many other incidents between the whites and the Cheyenne, at this place called Sand Creek.

For Mochi, it all began in the Time of the Freezing Moon (November), when she was putting wood on her lodge fire. In the distance she could hear the pony herds acting up, while the dogs in the village began barking as though something was about to happen. The sound was ever so soft at first, as though the wind's rhythm with mother earth had broken the serenity of that morning.

Mochi's mother, who was preparing the morning meal, heard it too. She thought it sounded like a large herd of buffalo nearby. It was Mochi's father, though, who hurried into the lodge and shouted, "Quick, come look outside!"

When they did, what they saw both frightened and held them in awe. On a ridge to the west of the village was a large group of white soldiers on horseback. They looked like a large blue *shi shi kneh woh ees* (snake) uncoiling over the ground, while steam from the breaths of both men and horses rose up, eerie and silent, like *mis tah yeots* (a mist of death) and then vanished towards morning's clear sky.

Mochi and her family were not the only ones who saw the soldiers. From their position in Bumping Wolf's (War Bonnet's) camp, they could see that old Chief White Antelope had also come out of his lodge, as had Moke Tavato (Black Kettle). These two called out to their people to remain calm. A U.S. flag was unfurled above Black Kettle's lodge and he raised a white flag to show the soldiers they were friendly, but this did not help. As the Cheyenne stared at this large body of men that almost completely surrounded their village, the earth all around them suddenly and violently began to shake with the roar of explosions. The soldiers had begun firing their big guns into the village.

Explosion after explosion ripped the Cheyenne lodges and people to pieces. Above the roar of those big guns, Mochi heard the screams of her people. Almost as quickly as the explosions came, she heard the sound of the soldiers above and around her beginning their charge.

People of all ages ran in panic. White Antelope began shouting in the language of the *vehos* (whites) "Stop! Stop!" but it was no use. Mochi watched as he folded his arms and began singing the Cheyenne Death Song. She then watched in horror as the first group of soldiers charged into the village. One of them rode up to White Antelope and shot the old chief down. This soldier then dismounted and scalped White Antelope and began cutting off his ears and private parts.

Before the Cheyenne had a chance to react, the soldiers were upon them from all sides of the village. They soon invaded Bumping

Wolf's camp, and Mochi watched, as if frozen in time, as her mother, father, and grandfather were all killed. Mochi's husband, Standing Bull, was also killed trying to protect her. Still in shock from the suddenness of the attack, Mochi knew that she must fight or die that day.

As if aided by some superhuman force, Mochi ran back into her lodge and grabbed her grandfather's buffalo gun. She shot at a soldier who was coming after her. Mochi then ran on, not knowing whether she had killed him or not. Through a thick haze of gunsmoke that now filled the village, she reloaded the buffalo gun and slowly fought her way through the center of the village towards the north. There, beyond the bloody and broken bodies of her people, lay the path to the dry creek bed. There, she thought, lay the safety of the sand hills. Until she got to the creek bed, Mochi did not know that the soldiers had lined both sides of it and were shooting everyone in sight. The creek bed was thickly littered with the bodies of old men, women, and children, mostly dead or dying. Behind Mochi was certain death, and she knew that to survive, she would have to make a run through that terrible maze of her people's bodies and the gauntlet of soldiers' bullets.

The frost-laden air burned Mochi's lungs as she ran; with each breath she took, the smell of death and gunpowder filled her nostrils. With each step she ran, Mochi felt the bullets pass by her body, as she watched those running with her suddenly drop in their tracks. Still armed, she ran west towards the sand hills' protection. Before she arrived, Mochi found a group of middle-aged Cheyenne men. They had organized what little firepower they possessed and made a short stand at this location until a cavalry troop overran their position. Fleeing from this new threat, the Cheyenne jumped into a dry stream bed above the camps. Before they could reach safety, however, they ran headlong into another company of cavalry. These soldiers opened fire on Mochi and the others as they rode up on the opposite bank of the stream.

After running two miles, Mochi finally reached the sand hills and began digging into the frozen earth alongside those who had arrived before her. Others who were there, although wounded, were digging as hard as those who were not. One young man had been shot through the hip. He probably would have bled to death that day had it not been so cold. His blood had frozen in his wound.

The Cheyenne worked furiously to dig into those hills. As they did, they were soon surrounded by more soldiers. By then the soldiers had worked themselves into a killing frenzy and they poured murderous fire into the Cheyenne defensive position. The Cheyenne stayed there until the cover of night. It was during this time that Mochi vowed revenge for the murder of her family and people. She had become a warrior that day and would forever remain a warrior. On that day she declared war on the *veho*. Mochi would take the fear she had experienced on that day and use it as a weapon against him. She had come to realize that the words White Antelope had sung in his death song were true: "Nothing lives long. Only the earth and mountains."

Black Kettle could not believe what was happening. After he had made a white flag of truce and hoisted it on his flagpole underneath "Old Glory," Chivington's men had ignored the gesture and charged down on him. Black Kettle grabbed his wife, Medicine Calf, and they ran for their lives. They too followed the same creek bed through the same gauntlet that Mochi and the others had barely survived. After a short while, Medicine Calf stopped and fell limp. She had been shot by the soldiers. Black Kettle saw that she did not move as the sickening "thud" sounds made by the bullets hitting her body continued. He wanted to stop, but knew any pause in his flight meant death. He continued his run up the creek to where his people had hidden in the pits.

When night came, the old chief crept out to where his wife had fallen. After thoroughly searching through the dead and dying, he found her—alive! Although she had been shot nine times, Medicine Calf clung tenaciously to life. Black Kettle carried her back to safety. Then he and Medicine Calf also vanished from the sight of Chivington's troops under cover of darkness to seek help.

Only the wind's sound broke nighttime's stillness as it moaned through the sage and prairie grass. The only other sounds penetrating that frozen night were made by the Cheyenne as those who had survived quietly escaped into the cold. There were almost no blankets or buffalo robes among them. They followed the direction of the Seven

Brothers of the Sky (the North Star of the Big Dipper). They knew that help lay there.

Little Bear and other warriors who were in Black Kettle's camp acted as a rear guard as the Cheyenne trudged through the cold, harsh safety of the prairie. They carried the wounded who could not walk. They dared not rest or light the fires they so desperately needed to warm themselves. They were unaware of what dangers lay ahead of or behind them. The wind and cold took no pity on the Cheyenne that night. Only their constant movement as they walked close together kept them from freezing to death. A terrible rage that burned within all who survived kept their spirits alive. Each step of their journey north ignited another reason to smoke the sacred pipe ... the occasion would be war.

The majority of Black Kettle's band thought only of revenge, and thoughts of war followed every step of their way to the South Fork of the Smoky Hill River, where they encountered outriders from the Cheyenne camp they sought, near a place called Bunch of Timbers. These villagers rushed food out to feed the exhausted Cheyenne, who had not eaten in almost three days. As they filled their empty stomachs, wood was thrown on the lodge fires to warm their frozen bodies. As the shock of their ordeal subsided, the Cheyenne vented their anger and frustrations on their own leaders. Many blamed Black Kettle for the massacre, because he was their chief. Around the council fires many Cheyenne howled Black Kettle down and removed him as chief. They elected Leg-in-the-Water in his place. Over time, though, the Cheyenne realized that Black Kettle's striving for peace and believing the white man were his only sins. Within six weeks, Black Kettle was again a Cheyenne chief. Leg-in-the-Water stayed with the clan, because there was no dishonor in anything he had done while he was chief. The Tsis Tsis Tas admitted they had made a mistake in removing Black Kettle.

After a few days of rest and recuperation, the Cheyenne moved northeast to the Solomon River in present-day Kansas, where the Sioux were encamped. From there, runners were sent across the Great Plains to other tribes of Sioux, Cheyenne, and Arapaho. Their message: assemble in council to talk of war against the whites.

Black Kettle voted for peace in the great council that followed, but many of the Cheyenne who gathered in this council, including Mochi, chose to fight the whites. Over the next eleven years, the five-foot, six-and-three-quarter-inch, 130-pound woman lived both a warrior's and a mother's life. She constantly engaged in war and raiding parties throughout Colorado, Nebraska, Wyoming, and Kansas. She also married a great war leader of the Bow Stringer Society named Medicine Water and gave birth to three of his children, all girls.*

Motherhood did little to slow Mochi down. She continued fighting alongside her husband, and during one great battle against the Pawnee, Mochi rode down amidst a group of enemy warriors and rescued her brother, who had had his horse shot out from under him. The Cheyenne called this battle "the time in which the girl saved her brother from the Pawnee." But the winds of fortune and time were running out for both Mochi and Medicine Water.

In mid-September 1874, Mochi and Medicine Water were roaming the Smoky Hill River area of western Kansas. On a hot late summer day, Mochi's war party attacked a white family named German en route to Colorado from Georgia. Mochi killed John German, his wife, and his oldest daughter. Cheyenne war customs forbade them to take any male prisoners. Two other women were killed in the initial attack. Their deaths were merciful compared to the ordeal the German's four remaining daughters endured. When word of the killings and the girls' abduction reached the army, Colonel Nelson Miles ordered his troops to step up their patrols. Until the German sisters were found and their kidnappers brought to justice, Miles would not let his troops or the hostiles rest. It was the beginning of the end for Mochi, Medicine Water, and the Cheyenne's last war in the southern plains.

Mochi and Medicine Water avoided capture for two months. They and their white captives suffered many hardships. Game was extremely scarce because the buffalo hunters of that era had all but exterminated

---

*The first born was named Red Woman. She died as a young woman. No one knows the cause of her death. The other two daughters were Standing Bird and Sprinkle Horse Woman; they lived to be very old.

the large herds. To Mochi, the appearance of Miles's pursuing troops seemed to replace the buffalo throughout the countryside. The Cheyenne were constantly on the run.

Finally, in April 1875, Mochi and the last holdouts of the warring Southern Tsis Tsis Tas surrendered at the Darlington Agency (near present-day El Reno, Oklahoma). Half starved and aged beyond her thirty-one years, Mochi's ordeal had not yet ended. The army considered her so dangerous that they ordered Mochi, Medicine Water, and twenty-nine other Tsis Tsis Tas to be chained and put in irons. Without trial or tribunal, the army transported them by train to St. Augustine, Florida, where they were imprisoned in a 300-year-old Spanish fort. It was here that Mochi and the others thought they had come to die.

Mochi sat in her jail cell awaiting death. She knew it was near. Here in this place, she had just seen the first of the Four Great Rivers the whites called oceans, and its overwhelming vastness lay just beyond her barred windows. The Cheyenne believed that when people died their *si yeouts* (spirit) must cross Four Great Rivers to reach the passage that led beyond the Milky Way to Seyan, the place of the dead. The salt spray and roar of the changing tides on the beach beyond the old Spanish fort's outer walls filled Mochi's every sense. She must have wondered about the other three rivers she would eventually cross. Mochi smelled Death's malevolent odor from every corner of her dank, mildewed cell. She was preparing herself for death. Had not her white soldier guards readied her for this journey by cutting off her long raven hair? Was this not the act of mourning to her people, the Tsis Tsis Tas? Yet Mochi had no fear of this journey. As a warrior she had escaped Death's ever-beckoning arms for years on the battlefields of the Great Plains. She had been preparing herself for this time since growing up in the land whites called Wyoming and Colorado, knowing that death comes to all.

From her small, damp cell, Mochi may have thought about death in this strange place. The Tsis Tsis Tas warriors believed that death in battle was acceptable, but in imprisonment was not. Mochi's new surroundings held no comfort for her mind or body. Only the nearness of her captured husband, Medicine Water, brought her peace.

Enduring chains and the degradation of being punished for speaking her own language, worshipping her own religion, or dressing in her native clothes, Mochi spent her three years of imprisonment. She was the only Native American woman in U.S. history to be sent to prison as a prisoner of war. Although they attempted to change her in all ways, the United States Army and the dank, damp cell that held her only succeeded in breaking her health: she contracted tuberculosis. They could not break her spirit.

Mochi and Medicine Water were released in 1878 and sent back to present-day Clinton, Oklahoma. Mochi died peacefully in 1881, surrounded by her family. She was buried on a high mound, thus securing her journey across the Four Great Rivers, leading her to the passageway across the Milky Way, to the place of the dead called Seyan. For those Tsis Tsis Tas who still tell the old tales, the memory of Mochi still lives. For it is said, "As long as your name is spoken, you will never die."

2

The Shadow on the Wall

On a prime business location on U.S. Highway 221 and North Carolina Highway 108, there is a brick building that remains empty most of the time. It seems every business that has occupied that land has failed for one reason or another. Some people in Rutherfordton, North Carolina will tell you it was due to bad management, or bad location, or some other "sound" business reason. But mostly you'll hear another explanation. Folks there will tell you the land is haunted and will remain so until something is done about the curse of Daniel Keith. You see, Daniel Keith was hanged in Rutherford County on December 11, 1880, for a crime he said he did not commit. He is said to have cursed the people and the land on the day they hanged him.

It all began many years earlier, when Daniel Keith first came to the county. Many folks feared the massive, six-foot, four-inch, 230-pound man. And few there would risk a confrontation with this notorious con man.

Keith's thirty-three years of life were a history of one con game after another, with petty theft as a side line. His life of crime began early, before he ever came to Rutherford County. He had conned many a man out of his money and women out of their favors. He was married three times and deserted all three wives. But nowhere in his criminal record was there ever a mention of his committing a violent crime.

Daniel Keith was born in Pulaski County, Kentucky, in 1848, the youngest child born of Clayborn Keith and his wife, Permillia. Clayborn was a farmer with a hundred dollars' worth of land. Life on the land was tough for the twenty-eight-year-old father of eight. Clayborn died thirteen years after Daniel's birth. The Civil War had broken out, and although Kentucky had not officially seceded from the Union, many of her native sons went to fight for the Confederacy. Keith was only fourteen at the time and his mother did her best to keep him home to help with the farm. But in 1862 the very large, muscular boy ran away from home. He possessed the "gift of gab" and had no problem convincing the Confederate Army he was of age to join. This was the beginning of his career as a criminal and he once said about it, "It was one of those critical points in a man's life at which there is but an inch between the path to heaven or the road to hell."

Keith soon deserted the army and made his way north to Indiana, where he began to steal on a small scale to survive. When he did find employment, he made a better living burglarizing his employers. When it got "too hot" for him in Indiana, he returned to Kentucky, stole a horse, and headed for Tennessee. While in Tennessee, he again joined the Confederate Army and again deserted it. This time he was caught, but again, through his smooth talking, escaped punishment.

After the war, Keith spent several years living and conning in Tennessee. In 1878 he moved southeast into North Carolina. Keith settled in Rutherford County and quickly made his presence known with a series of petty thefts and swindles.

Rutherford County was an ideal location for these con games and swindles, for it was an area in which gold could still be found. In 1831, the first dollar gold piece in U. S. history was minted in Rutherfordton, at Bechtler's Mint. Many of the area's men still dreamed of finding the "bonanza" that would assure them a rich and cozy life. Men of this nature proved to be easy pickings for Daniel Keith.

His biggest swindle took place in 1879, when he took a sixty-eight-pound rock and rubbed it with brass. He sold this "gold strike" to many a man in western North Carolina, making him one of the most hated men in the region. Many a victim swore he would get even with Keith. In January 1880, a tragedy would give these men the opportunity to rid Rutherford County of Daniel Keith once and for all.

The body of twelve-year-old Alice Ellis was found in a wooded area of the county. She had been brutally murdered. When Sheriff N. E. Walker was notified, a witness came forth and said he'd seen Daniel Keith in the area, and that he was "drunk and had blood on his shirt. He seemed real belligerent."

Within an hour of Sheriff Walker's leaving the crime scene, he contacted Keith at his cabin. Keith was sober, but there were bloodstains on his shirt. The experienced lawman coolly asked the massive man standing in front of him, "Where the blood come from, Daniel?"

Curious about the question, but without hesitation, Keith replied, "I've been skinning rabbits."

"Where they at?"

"The rabbits? Follow me Sheriff, they're hanging up over here behind the cabin."

With no idea what was going on, Keith led the sheriff to where the rabbit carcasses were hanging. He also showed him the skins he had stretched out to tan.

Putting his hand on his gun, and not taking his eyes off the man he was confronting, Sheriff Walker said, "We got a problem, Dan. Little Alice Ellis was murdered earlier today and some folks say they saw you in the area. What have you got to say for yourself?"

Astonished, Keith turned to the sheriff and coldly asked, "You sayin' I killed the girl? Walker, I've done a lot of things in my life, but murder ain't never been one of them. Folks around here stay clear of me even if I done 'em wrong. You know that."

"I know that, but this time I got a little girl that's been brutally murdered and a witness that says they saw you in the area. I'm taking you in until I get to the bottom of this." With that said, the sheriff asked the huge man, "Am I gonna have any trouble from you?"

Seeing Sheriff Walker's hand on his gun, Daniel Keith knew that if he tried to fight or run, he'd end up dead. "No, Sheriff, I won't give you any trouble, but you gotta swear you won't let any of these folks around here come visit me in the night before I go to trial."

"You've got my word on it."

Peacefully, the huge con man and swindler surrendered to Sheriff Walker and was put in the Rutherford County Jail to await trial. But the angry people of the county soon turned violent. Word had gotten out about Alice Ellis's murder and Keith's arrest. An angry mob was soon milling around outside the jail. Sheriff Walker saw what was happening and sent a deputy off on a fast horse to the neighboring Cleveland County Jail in Shelby, North Carolina, thirty miles away. The sheriff knew he didn't have the manpower to hold back a lynch mob and he didn't particularly want to shoot some of his friends over the likes of Daniel Keith. But he was a man of his word and he wasn't going to give up his prisoner to anybody before a trial could be held. He knew the sheriff in Shelby would house his prisoner. He'd done the same for him a couple of years earlier under the same circumstances. Both men knew that lynch mobs were highly unlikely to travel thirty miles to break somebody out of jail.

Daniel Keith was transferred to Shelby, North Carolina, within twenty-four hours of his arrest, and there he stayed until the spring term of the Rutherford County Court. The trial took a very bizarre turn. Although evidence was presented by the defense about the rabbits, in those days there was no scientific way to differentiate rabbit blood from human blood. Also, a witness testified that he'd seen an escaped convict from neighboring McDowell County in the area of the murder. This same convict was awaiting execution for committing the same crime of raping and killing a young girl in that county. The evidence was ruled inadmissible because of a ruling in North Carolina (*State vs. Baxter*) that "on trial of an indictment for crime, evidence tending to the guilt of another in its commission does not disprove the criminality of the party charged." Daniel Keith's luck had run out. He was found guilty of murder in the first degree.

He appealed his conviction all the way to the North Carolina Supreme Court, but it was sustained. Judge W. I. Love's sentence was, "That on December 11, 1880, Daniel Keith, you will be taken to a place of execution and there you will be hanged until you are dead, dead, dead."

A few days before Daniel Keith's execution, he was returned to the Rutherford County Jail. There he was "chained with a heavy chain to the bottom of the cage in which he was confined. ... His coffin was placed near the cage and near the place where he sat."

A couple of days before Keith was to hang, a reporter from the *Charlotte Observer* spoke with Keith at length. He told the reporter about his life and petty crimes, but vehemently proclaimed his innocence.

On December 11, 1880, Sheriff Walker took the shackled prisoner out of his cell and placed him in a wagon. About a half mile from the jail was a beautiful, wooded meadow (where the Rutherford County Hospital now stands). In the middle of the area was a hill. On this hill the scaffold had been built, and the locals called the place "The Hanging Meadow." A large crowd had gathered, including the reporter from the *Charlotte Observer.* On that gray December day, what many would consider a somber event had almost a carnival atmosphere. People brought their children and picnic baskets to the starkness of winter's barren trees and brown grass. As Sheriff Walker led the prisoner up to the gallows, a loud cheer rose from the crowd. Those who had been cheated by this man could now watch him hang.

Now the time came for the sheriff to ask the condemned man for his last words. Standing above the large crowd, the massive Keith, in a loud voice, said, "A man should be hung for what he's done, not for what he ain't done. And I say to all you gathered here today to watch me hang, the soul of an innocent man won't ever rest until he can prove himself innocent." There was silence following those words. Sheriff Walker was visibly shaken as he placed the rope around Daniel Keith's neck. He'd never hanged anyone before. Daniel, noticing this, said to the sheriff, "Keep a cool head. Don't get excited." At 1:00 in the afternoon the scaffold floor dropped beneath Daniel Keith's feet and he was hanged to death. The reporter there later wrote, "The world is rid of a monster."

But was it? A few days after the execution, something began to happen that to this day has never been explained. Folks passing the south side of the jail began to see something. There, on that south jail wall, was a shadow of sorts. As each day passed it took on a definite shape. It looked like the shadow of a large man being hanged. A large man with a beard. At first Sheriff Walker thought that this was some sort of stupid prank. There was nothing there to cause such a shadow to appear. Most likely, he thought, under the cover of darkness someone had come out and painted that shadow. He had his deputy cover the shadow with white paint, but within days the shadow had returned! Exactly where it had been before, only this time much more detailed and darker. Time and again they tried to paint over the shadow, but it always returned. The townspeople and the sheriff began to wonder if Daniel Keith's curse was coming true. At one point the sheriff tried to grow ivy up the south wall; it flourished everywhere except for where that shadow was. The shadow seemed to be more visible to some folks than to others, as though it were there to torment them. For eighty years thereafter many attempts were made to paint and whitewash the shadow away. Each time the shadow returned. Professional painters in the late 1950s took on the shadow. They felt that if they could get rid of it their reputations would flourish, but the shadow always returned. Every business that occupied the old jail building also failed. Finally, in 1960, the people of Rutherfordton removed the shadow by tearing down the old jail. They knew it wouldn't and couldn't come back now. The curse was over! But they were wrong!

The townspeople put a brick building on the location of the old jail. It was well built, but soon the new tenants of the building began complaining about strange occurrences there. Things like the new roof leaking when there was no reason for it, or the noises that seemed to come out of the walls. Ever since the new building was placed on that location, businesses ranging from fast food restaurants to used car lots to video game rooms have all gone bankrupt. The old people of Rutherford County will tell you, "It's the curse of Daniel Keith. It's still upon the land until he can prove himself innocent!"

The Medal and the Lady

The Mary Edwards Walker Story

S he was only twenty-nine years old in 1861, when the War Between the States broke out. But Mary Edwards Walker was already an oddity at this age because she was one of the first women physicians in the entire United States.

Six years earlier, Dr. Walker had graduated from Syracuse Medical College. She was a gentle and caring doctor who was about to create a storm of controversy that continues to this day.

When the war began, Dr. Walker applied for a commission in the Union Army as a surgeon. She was refused. According to a Union general, Mary couldn't be an army doctor. She was a woman. And everybody knew a woman couldn't be a doctor! But Mary argued that she was already a doctor and had been practicing medicine very successfully for almost six years. The army said again, "Mary, you can't be a doctor, you're a woman! Commission denied!"

Mary Walker was told, though, that if she wanted to, she could work at the Washington, D.C., hospital as a volunteer. So she did just that and worked there for nine months until 1862.

Undaunted in her quest to receive a commission, Mary Walker boldly presented herself to Major General Ambrose Burnsides (for whom "sideburns" were named). Dr. Walker was again denied a commission, but was told she could work as a field surgeon, again only as a volunteer.

For the next two years, Dr. Walker could be found driving an ambulance at the front lines, caring for the wounded, sick, and dying. She was easy to spot in her "uniform." She wore the gold-striped pants of an army officer and around her waist was a green sash signifying her status as a surgeon. On her head, she wore a large straw hat topped off with an ostrich plume.

Time after time, Dr. Walker risked life and limb in the thick of battle in places such as Fredericksburg and Chickamaugua.

After two years of combat service, Dr. Mary Edwards Walker again applied for a commission as a medical officer in the United States Army. She was again denied by an Army Medical Board in Chattanooga, Tennessee. The board stated in their review that, as a woman, she was "utterly unqualified for the position of medical officer," but Dr. Walker could continue to work as a volunteer.

Shortly after her rejection for being "utterly unqualified," Dr. Walker was appointed assistant surgeon to the 52nd Ohio Infantry by General George H. Thompson after the death of their previous doctor. In effect, Dr. Mary Walker became the first woman to become a commissioned officer.

Aside from her medical work on the battlefield, Dr. Walker may have done some spying for the Union. Army memos mentioned her "secret services" for the North.

After being in the 52nd for about a month, Dr. Walker was captured by Southern forces and sent to a prison in Richmond, Virginia. Four months later, one of her greatest triumphs took place. She was traded "man for man" for a Confederate officer during a prisoner exchange.

Dr. Walker's triumph was short lived. After her release, she was "refused" battlefield duty, but she was given her back pay and $100 a month to be a contract physician. The army refused to honor her commission with the 52nd Ohio Infantry.

Dr. Walker spent the rest of the war in Kentucky and Tennessee practicing medicine at a female prison and an orphanage. Inmates and staff alike were offended by Dr. Walker's gruff manner. The war had changed her, as it had millions of others who had witnessed the horrors of our most bloody war.

After the war, Dr. Walker was paid in full, but she was repeatedly refused her commission. She petitioned the White House so frequently that finally President Andrew Johnson asked Secretary of War Stanton if there was something he could do to recognize this woman's service. Mary Walker was becoming a presidential-sized headache.

Secretary Stanton ordered that in January 1866, Dr. Mary Edwards Walker would receive the Congressional Medal of Honor for services "above and beyond the call of duty."

Mary Edwards Walker, Congressional Medal of Honor recipient and attending physician at some of the bloodiest fighting in the history of this country, was about to embark on another journey for human rights, this time on the home front.

Dr. Walker started wearing pants in public, unheard-of behavior at that time. She found trousers very comfortable. She had worn them for years on the battlegrounds. So she continued to wear them in civilian life on the streets of Oswego, New York.

This led to another first: she was the first recipient of the Congressional Medal of Honor to be arrested! Her crime was "impersonating a man." Her personal choice of clothing was considered a crime, and after frequent arrests for her dress, Mary Walker went to trial. Forcefully and yet eloquently, Dr. Walker declared to the court her right "to dress as I please in free America on whose tented fields I served for four years the cause of human freedom." The courtroom cheered wildly and the judge ordered the police never to arrest her on a charge like that again.

Mary Walker continued to fight for many causes, which hurt her private practice. She crusaded for women's rights and in so accidentally started the U.S. Postal Service's present-day system of certified mail. When she tried to mail letters to different women's organizations, the Post Office would purposely lose them. If the letters were lost, this female troublemaker couldn't contact those other troublemakers. So, one day she showed up at the Post Office with her letters and a slip of paper. She made the postal clerk sign it, thus making him responsible for those letters reaching their destination.

Dr. Walker also crusaded against smoking (as a doctor she felt it was hazardous to one's health). She was also opposed to capital punishment.

Mary Walker finally was reduced to living off her pension, but she nearly lost it in 1901. She outraged the entire city of Oswego, New York, by asking for clemency for the anarchist who had just assassinated President William McKinley.

Dr. Walker's will to fight never diminished as old age started taking its toll. She continued to petition the army for her "lost" commission, without success.

In 1916, the Congress of the United States changed the rules about who could receive the Congressional Metal of Honor. One of these rules was that the person had to be on active duty in the armed forces of the United States.

Mary Edwards Walker had been considered a "contract surgeon" during the war, and she was notified that she was no longer eligible to wear her medal or receive its benefits. She ignored the order to not wear her medal and again started her crusade to regain her commission.

She personally appealed to congressmen and War Department officials, to no avail. On one of her frequent trips to Washington, D.C., she fell on the Capitol steps. Dr. Walker never recovered and on February 21, 1919, she died at the age of eighty-six.

Dr. Mary Edwards Walker was dead, but she was not forgotten. At the urging of a descendant, Dr. Walker's Congressional Medal of Honor was restored almost sixty years after its revocation. To this day she remains our nation's sole female recipient of the Congressional Medal of Honor.

Mary Edwards Walker was a remarkable woman. She was an activist whose causes are still being fought for: women's rights, smoking bans, and abolishment of capital punishment. She was the first and only woman recipient of the Congressional Medal of Honor. She was the first Congressional Medal of Honor recipient to be arrested. Mary Walker was the first woman to be commissioned as a medical officer and recognized as a surgeon in the United States Army. Long live her memory!

Ten Interesting Facts
about the Congressional Medal of Honor

1. The only man to win two Congressional Medals of Honor (CMH) in the Civil War was a man named Custer! Not George Armstrong Custer, but his younger brother Tom who, along with brothers Boston and George, a brother-in-law, and a nephew, died at the Battle of the Little Big Horn on June 25, 1876.

2. The only father and son team to win the CMH was Arthur MacArthur and his son, Douglas MacArthur. Both men received the medal for disobeying direct orders and both reached the highest rank the United States Army could bestow. Douglas was only one of four "five star" generals in the history of our country.

3. Probably the most infamous incident in the CMH's history occurred in December 1890, when soldiers of the 7th Cavalry, Custer's old command, brutally massacred mostly unarmed Lakota men, women, and children at Wounded Knee, South Dakota. Eighteen of these soldiers were given the CMH for this slaughter.

4. President Theodore Roosevelt was nominated for the CMH for his part in charging up San Juan Hill in Cuba during the Spanish American War. He never received the medal, but his name appears on the Medal's honor roll (Theodore Roosevelt, Jr., his son) for actions above and beyond the call of duty during the D-Day landings in Normandy in World War II.

5. The great showman, frontiersman, pony express rider, and buffalo hunter Buffalo Bill Cody won the CMH during the Cheyenne wars when he killed Yellow Hand. His medal was also taken from him by the same congressional action that removed Mary Walker's, because he was a civilian scout. In 1994, his medal was reinstated by an act of Congress sponsored by Wyoming Senator Alan Simpson.

6. The first African American soldier to receive the CMH was Sergeant William H. Carney of the 54th Massachusetts Colored Infantry, on July 18, 1863, for his participation in charging Fort Wagner, South Carolina during the Civil War. He wasn't given the Medal of Honor until 1900, thirty-seven years after the fact.

7. In 1875, ten Apache scouts who served with Lieutenant Colonel George Crook in his 1872–1873 winter campaign against the Apaches received the CMH.

8. During World War I, on October 8, 1918, Corporal Alvin C. York single-handedly killed twenty-five German soldiers, silenced thirty-five machine guns, and captured 132 German prisoners. He was the war's most famous hero. What isn't commonly known about "Sergeant" York is that in the late 1950s the U.S. government tried to take his Tennessee home away from him for back taxes. The people of Tennessee rallied behind their hero, and Sergeant York was able to keep his home. Throughout his life Alvin York was haunted, both in dreams and spirit, by the horrors of war.

9. In the 1992 presidential elections, third-party candidate Ross Perot's choice for vice-president was Rear Admiral James Stockdale, USN Retired. Many political pundits made fun of Perot's choice. But had they served with him as a prisoner of war in the Hanoi Hilton during the Vietnam War, their outlook would have been much different. A navy pilot,

Stockdale was shot down over North Vietnam in September 1965. From 1965 until his release in January 1973, Stockdale was severely beaten and tortured by his prison guards for creating ingenious ways of communicating with fellow prisoners, creating a chain of command, and keeping up morale. He risked his life time and again for his fellow American prisoners and received the CMH on March 4, 1976.

10. The last CMH was awarded by President Ronald Reagan on February 24, 1981, to Retired Master Sergeant Roy Benevidez for action in Vietnam in 1968. Benevidez was so severely wounded after saving numerous lives at the risk of his own that an army doctor thought he was dead. Although he could not speak or move while about to be toe tagged, Benevidez could spit, and that's exactly what he did, at the doctor. Benevidez slowly recovered from his wounds and was medically discharged from the army. He was awarded the CMH only after people who thought he was dead found out that he was in fact still alive. In late November 1998, Benevidez died at the age of sixty-three. He was buried with full military honors at Arlington National Cemetery.

4

Nathan's Legacy

He wasn't able to leap tall buildings in a single bound. But it is said that he could lift a full-grown horse by himself and outrun, out-jump, and outfight any man in western North Carolina. His exploits won the admiration of all those who saw him and everyone was in awe of this six-foot, six-inch, 250 pound man of rock hard muscle.

The old timers say that he was one heck of a man, this blacksmith who could swing a ten-pound hammer with each hand. In the years preceding the War Between the States, in Kane River area of Yancy County, North Carolina, Nathan Dempsey became a legend.

He lived in a time when men cleared the land with horse-drawn plows and muscle and sweat, when trees were felled with axes and handsaws, when logs were split with hammers and wedges. It was a time when men hunted and grew their own food.

In those days—long before the rise of football and baseball—running and jumping contests were among the most popular sporting events. But the main attractions were the fights held on Saturday afternoons.

By nature, Nathan was a quiet, caring man who later became a devoted husband and father. But when it came to fighting, no one who ever got hit by one of Nathan's huge fists thought of him as a "gentle" man. For years he could defeat any man in any event he entered. He excelled in fighting and wrestling. But this excellence would eventually cause Nathan some problems.

It was a Saturday afternoon. Eight very large men were waiting to challenge the champion of Yancy County to a fighting match. The hot summer afternoon seemed cool compared to the heated excitement of the crowd. They knew that this new group of men—hunters, woodsmen, and stone masons—were the cream of the crop of the Carolina fighters, each eager to win a reputation and a purse of coins by defeating the "Blacksmith from Burnsville."

One by one they entered the ring. One by one they were soundly defeated. Losing was more than their pride could bear, so they made plans for later that afternoon. Each knew he couldn't beat Nathan alone, so they decided they would collectively jump the blacksmith and teach him a lesson he'd never forget.

Nathan saw them coming. As if aided by supernatural force, he threw his attackers off as if they were rag dolls. On their first assault, they were heaved in every direction, landing in dirt and mud. On their second and last assault, Dempsey decided to teach them a lesson. When the dust cleared, eight men had been thrown into a chicken coop. The champion of Yancy County proved beyond all doubt that he was still champion.

This was the last time Nathan fought. The losers were not about to give up. They went to the sheriff and complained that Nathan had attacked them without provocation. They demanded that something be done.

The sheriff went to Nathan and, without giving him a chance to explain his side of the story, told him that if he ever used his hands for fighting again, he would be arrested. As far as the people of the county were concerned, Nathan's massive hands were "unlawful weapons."

As far as can be determined, Nathan never did fight again. He moved up to what is now West Virginia and faded into a life of obscurity. Nathan married and started a family of his own. He had a son, Hirum. It was said by those who knew him that Hirum was the opposite of his father in physical stature and that he was a meek, mild-mannered person.

In the late 1880s, Hirum Dempsey headed west to the Rocky Mountains in search of a fortune in the goldfields. He settled down and opened a mercantile store and later taught school in a mining town in southwestern Colorado. He married, and in 1896 Hirum's wife bore him a son. They named him William Harrison.

Young William grew up in the rough and tumble atmosphere of a mining town. In order to survive his childhood nickname of "Sissy Willy," he learned how to fight. One day a boy who was a head taller and twenty pounds heavier than Willy started picking on him. When Willy could take it no more he punched his larger opponent right between the eyes and he dropped like a stone. It took the local veterinarian fifteen minutes to revive the would-be bully. Like his grandfather and unlike his father, William had a natural talent for fighting. With his mother's encouragement, he later turned his natural ability into a profession.

William fought in mining towns and camps all over Colorado, Utah, and Nevada. He took on all challengers. Some say that he inherited grand-daddy Nathan's punching power. William's ring opponents claimed his fists should have been considered "unlawful weapons."

William would also become a legend in his lifetime. His exceptional fighting ability and tenacious style earned him a nickname that included the Colorado town in which he was born. He was known to the world as "Jack Dempsey, the Manassa Mauler," Heavyweight Champion of the World from 1919 to 1926.

It has been said that William "Jack" Dempsey was the legacy left to the boxing world by his grandfather Nathan, the "Blacksmith from Burnsville." The exploits of Jack Dempsey, one of the greatest heavyweight champions of all time, have been chronicled in newspapers and films all over the world. But only stories handed down by word of mouth from generation to generation have preserved the memories of Nathan Dempsey, a real legend.

Dempsey Shorts

1. In 1980, two young muggers accosted a dapperly dressed elderly man who was about to enter a cab in the streets of New York City. Before they knew what had happened, they found themselves flat on their backs on the sidewalk. The eighty-five-year-old-man they had just tried to mug was Jack Dempsey. Even though he was sixty years older than when he first won the heavyweight championship of the world, he still had incredible speed and punching power in his fists. Without any fanfare, Dempsey entered the taxi and told the astonished driver to drive him to his restaurant.

2. Jack Dempsey started his professional boxing career at the age of nineteen using the name Kid Blackie. Within five years he had fought over eighty professional fights.

3. In 1923, during a title match against the heavyweight champion of Argentina, Luis Angel Firpo, Dempsey was knocked completely out of the ring in the first round. He immediately climbed back into the ring and in the second round knocked Firpo out.

4. Jack Dempsey was the most popular heavyweight champion from 1919 on into the 1940s (even though he quite fighting title bouts in 1927). He was so popular that he became the first fighter in boxing history to attract five $1 million gates.

5

Mother Maggard

During Colorado's gold rush days, there were many stories of white settlers' first meetings with Indians. Some were tragic, others touching. One incident involved an older woman named "Mother Maggard," who had "a head full of carrot colored hair, loose fitting store bought teeth and an abundance of homeliness" and a group of curious Arapaho she horrified.

Like many of the gold rushers, Mother Maggard came to Colorado to seek her fortune. She found it in her talents as a cook. Her idea of being Colorado's first food delivery service met with instant success. She would take unprepared food in her wagon full of pots and pans, go into the mining camps, and cook homestyle meals for the miners, who in turn paid her quite well.

One spring day in 1860, near the outskirts of Denver, a peaceful hunting party of Arapaho heard loud, clanging noises. As they approached the top of a knoll, they discovered its source. It was Mother Maggard's wagonload of pots and pans.

Seeing the Arapaho and fearing an imminent attack, the men in Mother Maggard's party immediately reached for their guns. Mother Maggard stopped them, reminding them that they were outnumbered five to one. She thought she could frighten the Arapaho off.

The first object Mother Maggard grabbed was a large frying pan. She grasped it by the handle and waved it around her head, screaming.

All she succeeded in doing was making the Arapaho more curious. Cautiously, they approached the wagon for a better look.

Seeing that her first attempt at scaring off the Arapaho was failing, Mother Maggard dropped the frying pan and reached for a large pot and ladle. The old woman then began to beat them together furiously while screaming at the top of her lungs. Again, she succeeded only in making the Arapaho more curious. Even more cautiously, the Arapaho ventured closer to this unusual sight. They had never seen such a homely woman acting in such a crazy way.

Mother Maggard was now at a total loss about what to do next. Thoughts of being killed or worse, being ravaged, raced through her mind. Out of desperation, she removed her loose-fitting false teeth and snapped them together with her hands at the astonished Arapaho. They had never seen false teeth before and fled in terror, leaving the old toothless woman standing laughing inside the wagon, with her four companions.

Mother Maggard returned to Denver with her companions and the tale immediately spread throughout the town of her chasing off a war party with her false teeth. The Arapaho went back to their village and told the people of a woman who could put teeth in her hands and try to bite them. Both stories are still being told in both cultures.

6

Silas Soule

A Forgotten Hero of Sand Creek

Two gunshots pierced the pleasant April night, momentarily silencing the throng of people in Denver's numerous saloons. For Silas Soule's bride of three weeks, the silence was deafening. When the city's pathways again filled with people, they shouted and ran towards the gunshot's source. There they discovered the body of Captain Silas Soule lying on a dust-covered walkway with a bullet in his brain. Ironically, he had predicted his own murder. And his untimely death gave birth to a legend in Colorado's history.

Where there are legends, there are heroes who are often born from tragedy, and the embryo from which they are conceived is adversity. In the twenty-six years of his life, Silas Soule's essence had been nourished by the milk of valor. Those who knew him understood that injustice and prejudice seared his soul and he feared neither death nor the threat of it in his quest to fight these vexations to mankind's existence. In the tradition of ancient heroes, Soule began his adventures long before he was a man.

Six years before the Civil War, Missouri border gangs ravaged the Kansas-Missouri border, committing murder, robbery, and arson. Their goal was to create a pro-slavery state of Kansas, while equally determined abolitionists sought to keep Kansas "a homestead of the free."

Murder begat murder, and soon raiders on both sides vehemently sought vengeance in a bloody prelude to civil war.

The clash between these two factions struck like a bolt of lightning during the spring of 1856. On May 21, a group of Missouri raiders sacked and burned Lawrence, Kansas, which "Free Staters" considered their center. Although Missouri raiders killed only two people, the consequences of the attack were grave. Three days later, a band of fanatical abolitionists led by John Brown found five pro-slavery settlers camped along the banks of Pottawatomie Creek. Brown and his men hacked them to pieces with artillery swords. That deed inflamed America's western frontier. Hatred, bloodshed, and an obsession for vengeance were its aftermath.

One year before Brown's raid, fifteen-year-old Silas Soule ventured west with his father, Amasa, from Boston. In Kansas Silas Soule became an active member of the "underground railroad." Armed with "Beecher's Bibles,"[1] Soule and other eastern abolitionists helped escaping slaves on their journey to freedom. They rode as "jayhawkers" throughout "bleeding" Kansas for almost five years. Silas Soule's prowess as a guerrilla raider was evident in 1859, when he and four others rescued famed underground "railroader" Dr. John Doy. Doy's conviction and sentence to five years' imprisonment for transporting runaway slaves to safety made it imperative for the abolitionists to act. The day before Doy's transfer to the Missouri State Prison, Soule's band broke into a St. Joseph jail and released him.

In the same year, after John Brown's capture at Harper's Ferry, Virginia, Soule became involved in a daring plan to break Brown out of prison. However, the attempt was never made, and Soule returned to the West. His adventures took him to the very hell holes of violence, yet he matured well beyond his nineteen years, and somewhere amidst the gunsmoke and dust of the Kansas frontier, he lost his youth.

---

[1] Beecher's Bibles were rifles that were paid for and shipped to the abolitionists with the blessings of the famous Brooklyn clergyman Henry Ward Beecher. Beecher's sister was Harriet Beecher Stowe, whose book *Uncle Tom's Cabin* helped ignite the debate on slavery in the United States.

From the Kansas plains to Colorado's goldfields, Silas Soule rode into manhood and history on a "stallion" called Destiny. Within the span of a single turbulent decade, that mythical "steed" that guides all men took him to Sand Creek on the 29th day of November 1864, to witness one of America's greatest tragedies: the Sand Creek Massacre. Only Soule and a handful of officers, out of 700 soldiers present, dared confront the man responsible, Colonel John Chivington, a former Methodist minister. Soule's meeting with Chivington wasn't his first, or his last.

These two men had met each other before, in 1860. Two years later both had participated in the Battle of Glorieta Pass in New Mexico. The young "jayhawker," then a lieutenant, served under then Major Chivington of the First Colorado Regiment. Both men fought valiantly and earned reputations for being fearless, but these two men had no fondness for each other. Chivington often used his massive size to intimidate those who disagreed with him, but Soule demonstrated time and again that he had no fear of the former preacher's bulk. The young captain defied Chivington on numerous occasions. Ironically, the former man of God had no ability to forgive his enemies or turn the other cheek. Soule and Chivington clashed one last, fatal time after Sand Creek. It began with a newspaper banner.

On December 30, 1864, the *Rocky Mountain News* carried the headline " 'High Officials' Spur Investigation." The paper recounted Major Edward Wynkoop's reports about Sand creek to Washington, D.C. This infuriated not only Washington officials, but almost the entire population of Denver. They directed their rage, not at Chivington and his troops, but at "High Officials" and Major Wynkoop! The same issue of the *News* printed the fabled reports and letters Chivington, Shoup, and Anthony had written. The paper questioned "who those 'high officials' were;" while many of the "Bloody Third" and their admirers stated with more than mild intention "that they had half a mind to 'go for them'." Threats spread throughout the city of stringing up those betraying the "boys of the Third."

In the following weeks, while the Queen City waited, officials were already in Denver and at Fort Lyon taking affidavits from those who had witnessed the "incident" at Sand Creek. To the dismay of "Bloody Third" members, an investigation had indeed begun and officials were questioning people about what they had seen and heard. They suspected that most of these men, including their leader Colonel Chivington, were glad they had mustered out of the army!

Two of the complainants were Major Edward Wynkoop and Captain Silas Soule. The "high official" turned out to be Colorado's Chief Justice Benjamin Hall. Others complaining to Washington were Indian Agent Samuel Colley and Lt. Colonel Samuel Tappan.

On January 8, 1865, from his wintry, isolated post at Fort Lyon, Soule wrote home to his mother, "I hope the authorities at Washington will investigate the killings of these Indians. I think they will be apt to hoist some of our high officials. I would not fire on the Indians with my Company and the Colonel said he would have me cashiered, but he is out of the service before me and I think that I stand better than he does in regard to his great Indian fight."[2] The day before Soule wrote this letter, the combined forces of the Sioux, Cheyenne, and Arapaho had sacked the town of Julesburg, Colorado.

In Washington, D.C., two days after Soule wrote home, the House of Representatives passed a motion "that the Committee on the Conduct of the War be required to inquire into and report all the facts connected with the late attack of the third regiment of Colorado volunteers, under Colonel Chivington, on the Cheyenne tribe of Indians, near Fort Lyon."[3] The inquiry's immediate action shocked those awaiting word of the investigation. It relieved some but outraged others.

Within less than two weeks after Soule wrote to his mother, the United States Army appointed him provost marshall of the district and transferred him to Denver. Five weeks later, he testified against Chivington in a military investigation.

As the investigation began to unfold, the frontier citizens of Denver split into two camps: pro-Chivington or pro-Wynkoop and

---

[2] Unpublished letter of Silas Soule, January 8, 1865.

[3] "Massacre of Cheyenne Indians," Transcript, U.S. Military Hearings, Denver, Colorado, April 1865, p. 3.

Soule. Those same citizens liked Wynkoop and Soule, especially Soule, because of his jovial, devil-may-care personality. But even folks who thought well of these men treated their charges against Chivington as something akin to heresy. Many in town looked upon the huge former preacher as a man larger than life. Wasn't he the man who helped bring God's word to the godless during Denver's infancy? And wasn't he the hero of Glorieta Pass? Wasn't it Chivington who promised protection for Colorado's citizens against slavery's sins and hostile attacks from "savages?"

Why would two brother officers do this to a man they had known and fought beside for years? Were they jealous of his victory over "500" Cheyenne and Arapaho "warriors?" Or were some of the other stories whispered in town really true, that maybe there were mostly women and children in the village at Sand Creek?

Soon the whispers were spoken aloud, then written down with pen and ink. In fact, whispers became sworn statements. In his affidavit, taken at Fort Lyon, John Smith gave a detailed account of his service as an interpreter and trader. In reference to Chivington's attack at Sand Creek, Smith, the man who probably knew the Cheyenne better than any white man alive save William Bent, stated, "When the troops first approached, I endeavoured to join them, but we was repeatedly fired upon, as also the soldier and the civilian with me. When the troops began approaching, I saw Black Kettle, the head chief, hoist the American flag over his lodge, as well as a white flag, fearing there might be some mistake as to who they were."[4]

Soon others began testifying about the atrocities committed against mostly women and children at Sand Creek. It sickened most of those who listened to learn that these atrocities were committed with the knowledge of Colonel John M. Chivington, and that he took no measures to prevent them.

From March 13 through March 15, 1865, the Congressional Committee on the Conduct of War held its first hearings. The committee called Governor John Evans, who was already in Washington, to

---

[4] *Ibid.,* p. 5.

testify first. As Territorial Governor, Evans was Superintendent of Indian Affairs. Through his testimony, he convinced Congress of one thing: He possessed no knowledge of plains Indians or their customs. Time and again, when asked about Cheyenne hierarchy, his answers were confused and contradictory. The Committee on the Conduct of War asked Evans, "Have you any knowledge of any acts committed by either of those chiefs [Black Kettle and White Antelope], or by the bands immediately under their control-any personal knowledge?"

Evans's answer was cut short when he replied, "In 1862, a party of these Dog Soldiers ..."

The chair of the committee interrupted Evans, stating, "I am not asking about the Dog Soldiers, but about Black Kettle's band."

Evans shot back, "They are the same Indians. The Dog Soldiers were a sort of vigilance committee under those old chiefs."

The Committee then reminded Evans, "I understood you to say, a few minutes ago that the Dog Soldiers threw off the authority of the old chiefs, and were independent of them."

One of the last questions the committee asked the governor was, "With all the knowledge you have in relation to these attacks and depredations by the Indians, do you think they afford any justification for the attack made by Colonel Chivington on these friendly Indians, under the circumstances under which it was made?"

The ever-political Evans's answer was noncommittal: "As a matter of course, no one could justify an attack on Indians while under the protection of the flag. If those Indians were under the protection of the flag, it would be a question that would be scarcely worth asking, because nobody could say anything in favor of the attack. I have heard, however—that is only a report—that there was a statement on the part of Colonel Chivington and his friends that these Indians had assumed a hostile attitude before he attacked them. I do not know whether that is so or not. I have said all I have to do with them. I suppose they were being treated as prisoners of war in some way or other."[5]

---

[5] *Ibid.*, p. 38.

Meanwhile, one month before Denver's congressional hearings commenced,[6] the Secretary of War appointed military officials to investigate the massacre. The commission appointed Lt. Colonel Samuel Tappan as its chair. Chivington, infuriated by this appointment, appealed to the board, stating, "Gentlemen, I would most respectfully object to Lieutenant Colonel S.F. Tappan, first veteran battalion Colorado cavalry, being a member of the commission, for the following reasons to wit:

"1st: That the said Lieutenant Colonel S.F. Tappan is and for a long time past has been, my open and avowed enemy.

"2nd. That the said Lieutenant Colonel S.F. Tappan has repeatedly expressed himself very much prejudiced against the killing of the Indians near Fort Lyon, Colorado Territory, commonly known as the battle of 'Sand Creek,' and has said that it was a disgrace to every officer connected with it, and that he [Tappan] would make it appear so in the end.

"3rd. That I believe, from a full knowledge of his character, that he cannot divest himself of his prejudices sufficiently to render an impartial verdict, and is, therefore, not such a judge as the law contemplates when it directs that all men shall be tried by an impartial tribunal."[7]

Chivington's objections were overruled after Tappan clarified his statements and his feelings about Chivington's actions.

Taking of testimony began on February 15, 1865. The first witness called to testify was Captain Silas Soule. Prior to his testimony, Soule received numerous death threats. True to his nature, he was not intimidated. As a result of the threats, he determined to fulfill his duty as an officer; the truth would be known one way or the other. At his opening testimony to the commission, Soule calmly answered questions about his name, age, rank, time in service, and the events leading

---

[6] Congressional hearings were being held in Denver and Washington, D.C., during the same time period.

[7] "The Sand Creek Massacre," Transcript, U.S. Congressional Hearings, Washington, D.C., March 1865, p. 5.

up to Sand Creek. He included his meeting with Chivington and his troops, two days before the massacre. The commission then adjourned until 9:30 the next morning.

February 16 was the seventh day of the hearing, but only the second day of testimony. For the very first time, the truth was being told, under oath, about the actual events that took place on November 29, 1864. For two and a half days, the commission questioned Soule in minute detail about the events he witnessed at Sand Creek. They also queried his observations on his return trip to the massacre site.

During those days, the massive Chivington glared at Soule and took notes. Then, on February 17 at 2:00 in the afternoon, Chivington took his turn to ask questions. Chivington, who gave no quarter at Sand Creek, showed no mercy during his cross-examination of Soule. The former colonel relentlessly probed Soule's testimony for any inconsistencies. Unshaken, the young captain again showed his nemesis he would not be bullied and survived Chivington's three days of torturous questioning. Lieutenant Crammer and Major Wynkoop both supported Soule's testimony, as did Old Jim Beckwourth, who had acted as a scout during the massacre.

Throughout this bizarre period in Denver's history, tempers flared and fights erupted in the streets between pro- and anti-Chivington camps. On two separate occasions, attempts were made on Silas Soule's life. Two weeks after Soule had finished his testimony against Chivington, the hearings were still in full swing. Ned Wynkoop advised his friend to be careful while in the streets. He knew the "Chivington people" would take revenge on all who defamed their leader. Soule appreciated the warnings, but the young captain already knew he was going to die.

The very marrow of courage is selfless aggression. And valor's pinnacle is often reached through truth's sometimes harsh eloquence. Within its annals, the cost of justice is often life itself. Soule treated his quest for justice as though it were for the Holy Grail. In the latter part of March, Soule and his friend Captain George Price decided to take advantage of a beautiful spring day. They hired a buggy and rode to Central City. They talked of many things, as young men do, including

Soule's new-found love, the daughter of rancher Charles Coberly. He asked his friend, George, to be the best man at his wedding. A more sobering conversation followed. Soule was also worried. He told Price of his overwhelming premonition of doom. He felt that his testimony against Chivington would cost him his life. He was not frightened by the Grim Reaper's afterworld. What scared him existed in the commission's hearings. He told Price he felt his "character would be assailed" and an attempt to destroy his testimony would be made.

George told his friend and comrade from the war-torn plains of Colorado that if Soule's prediction came true, he would fight those persons questioning his character. The two young warriors made a pact: the truth about Sand Creek would be heard and documented for all time! Within thirty days, Silas Soule was dead.

Before his death, however, Soule did experience love's ecstasy. He married and, as promised, his friend George Price stood up as his best man. It all ended on an April night three weeks later. The weather was surprisingly pleasant for that time of year. A slight breeze breathed its way into Denver on its journey from the plains. Only the cottonwood trees standing their lone vigil along the Platte River's banks felt its touch as it quietly entered the city. Most of Denver's good citizens were indoors, at home or visiting with friends.

Between 9:30 and 10:00 on the last night of his life, Silas Soule and his new bride returned home to Curtis Street from visiting friends. After they had been inside a short time, a number of "shots were fired in the upper part of the city, evidently to decoy him out and the Captain started to ascertain the cause. While passing along Lawrence Street, near F, and directly in front of the residence of Dr. Cunningham, he seems to have been met by the assassin and the indications are that both men fired at the same instant."[8] Silas Soule lay dead with a bullet in his brain. Evidence at the scene, though, indicated that Soule had wounded his assassin. The killer had dropped his gun and left a distinct, bloody trail leading away from the murder scene towards the military camp.

---

[8] Patrick M. Mendoza, *Song of Sorrow: Massacre at Sand Creek* (Denver, CO: Willow Wind Publishing, 1993).

The city streets quickly filled with people and patrols were ordered out to find the provost marshall's killer. The murder of the likable and capable Silas Soule shocked the entire town. John Walley, the city's undertaker, carried Soule's lifeless body with reverence to his mortuary. This solemn occasion would not be profaned by anyone.

Soule's funeral services were held three days later. His widow, friends, and fellow officers attended and the church overflowed with mourners. Even Governor Evans came and paid his respects. Only Chivington and his followers were conspicuous by their absence. This break with military tradition was reinforced the very next day, when the commission reconvened.

Chivington introduced an affidavit taken from a teamster named Lipman Meyer.[9] He read from a lengthy deposition taken at Fort Lyon accusing Captain Silas Soule of drunkenness in the line of duty, theft, and cowardice. Upon hearing these ludicrous charges against his recently slain friend, Captain George Price angrily made an objection to the commission, saying the accusations in Meyer's deposition had nothing to do with the incident at Sand Creek. Price told the commission Meyer's deposition was nothing more than an attempt to blacken the name and reputation of a man who fought for his country. The young captain also reminded commission members that Soule's only "sin" was courage, and it took a great deal of it to make a stand against the injustices done to the Cheyenne and Arapaho people by Colonel John M. Chivington! George Price kept his pact with his friend, and Chivington's efforts to disqualify Silas Soule's testimony were in vain. Over the vehement protests of Chivington, the commission agreed with Price's objection and Lipman Meyer's deposition was not received as evidence.

As the hearings continued, the Cheyenne, Arapaho, and Sioux waged their war against the whites. Their war, however, was not confined to Colorado alone. The Southern Cheyenne's pilgrimage into Wyoming and South Dakota in the spring of 1865 went almost unnoticed. There, they banded together for the first time in almost forty years with their cousins, the Northern Cheyenne, and with tribes of the Sioux

---

[9] "The Sand Creek Massacre," p. 187.

nation. This joining of forces went unnoticed because of what was happening 2,000 miles away in the East, in the land of the "Great White Father."

On April 9, 1865, Robert E. Lee surrendered to Ulysses S. Grant. It was Palm Sunday and the Union was again united. Five days later, John Wilkes Booth assassinated President Abraham Lincoln at Ford's Theatre in Washington, D.C. It was the first time in American history a president had been murdered. Within days of this tragedy, the army cornered Lincoln's killer in a Maryland barn and killed him. Lincoln's successor, Andrew Johnson, was a Southerner and rumored to be an alcoholic. The nation's democracy teetered on the very brink of anarchy.

Those resounding events in history muffled the gunshots piercing the pleasant night of April 23, when a young man was killed in the streets of Denver. But through the tales of his deeds he was raised into legend's netherland, like the ancient ones before him called "heroes."

Theodosia

A Lady Lost

Out of the mists of time, located somewhere between the earth and sky, up close to the edge of your imagination, there dwells a place where legends are born. On December 30, 1812, one such legend began when Theodosia Burr Alston and everyone aboard the schooner *Patriot* sailed from Georgetown, South Carolina, out of the pages of history and into that oblivion man calls "legend." There have been many versions of what actually happened to that ship, but to this day little proof exists to substantiate any of them. Although the facts of Theodosia Burr Alston's life are not nearly as interesting as those of her father, Aaron Burr, her disappearance remains one of the great mysteries in American history.

Theodosia's father, Aaron Burr, was the vice-president of the United States during Thomas Jefferson's first administration. Even though he was twice tried and acquitted of treason, he is still best remembered as the man who killed Secretary of the Treasury, Alexander Hamilton, in a famous duel. In the Outer Banks of North Carolina, Hamilton is fondly remembered as the man who obtained the monies for the construction of the first Cape Hatteras lighthouse. Although the present lighthouse (the tallest in the United States) is the second to stand at this location, the old-timers of this area still call it the Hamilton Light in his honor.

After his second trial for treason, Aaron Burr left this country for England in political disgrace, leaving behind his only child, Theodosia. Before he departed however, the ever-ambitious Burr had introduced his daughter to Joseph Alston. Alston came from a very wealthy and prominent Southern family. After a lengthy courtship, Theodosia, the New York socialite, married Joseph Alston, Southern gentleman.

Following the marriage, Theodosia Alston moved with her husband to his plantation, The Oaks, near present-day Murrell's Inlet, South Carolina. Joseph Alston also purchased a home for his wife in Charleston at 94 Church Street.

The Alstons lived in comfort and happiness for the first few years of their marriage, even though Joseph had been elected governor of South Carolina. They had a son, whom Theodosia named after her father, but at the age of ten, Aaron Burr Alston died of a fever. It was said by some, but denied by others, that Theodosia suffered a nervous breakdown because of the loss of her only child and a great loneliness from being away from her father and New York. Theodosia's separation from her father soon ended. When the War of 1812 began, Aaron Burr returned to his United States.

Theodosia Alston made plans to return to New York for a lengthy visit with her father. During this period, she commissioned a portrait of herself and had it framed in a gold leaf frame. It was a gift for her father. On that fateful December day, Theodosia boarded the *Patriot* with her portrait in Georgetown, South Carolina, and sailed for New York to see her father. It is at this point that the facts begin to fade and the legends begin to grow.

The *Patriot* sailed north on her course towards New York into a coastal area of North Carolina known as the Outer Banks. What happened next has been the subject of numerous theories.

The history of this area is unique because here the uncommon is commonplace, from the disappearance of the first English colony and its inhabitants on Roanoke Island in 1584 to the first airplane flown by the Wright Brothers at Kitty Hawk (the actual location was at a place called Kill Devil Hill). It was a wild and desolate place of haunting beauty that has slowly given way to the encroachment of modern hotels, beach homes, condominiums, and shopping malls. The coastline of these islands is still known as the "Graveyard of the Atlantic" because more than 648 ships have either wrecked, run aground, or disappeared here. The bottom of the sea here is all sand. What is deep water one day can be shallow soon after and the storms that frequent the area can be deadly to those at sea and on land.

One story about Theodosia Alston's disappearance says that the *Patriot* and all souls on board vanished in a terrible storm off the coast of Cape Hatteras, but there are other persistent tales that the ship was taken by pirates.

To this day, the inhabitants of the islands refer to themselves as "bankers." They are a hearty breed and very proud of their heritage. At one time, though, these islands of Cape Hatteras, Ocracoke, and an area called Nag's Head were infested with pirates. The most famous of these was none other than Edward Teach, better known to the world as Blackbeard.

Many of the other inhabitants of these islands had no ships to plunder those at sea, but they were ingenious "land pirates." These cutthroats' favorite trick was to tie red and green lanterns on a horse and walk it up and down the beach on a starless night. An unsuspecting ship would think it was another ship and would be lured aground. Once the ship was aground, these pirates would then take their rowboats out, board the ship, and kill the ship's company and all her passengers. Then they would make away with the cargo and the victims' valuables.

One story about Theodosia Alston says that the *Patriot* fell into the hands of the pirates near Cape Hatteras and all aboard were made to walk the plank. It was said that Theodosia Alston was the last to die, bravely walking the plank with outstretched arms. It was also said that her portrait was taken to the island as part of the loot and was found some years later in a shack.

A second story says that Theodosia Alston was the sole survivor of that pirate attack. She survived because, having recently recovered from the loss of her child, and after watching all of the other people on the ship being brutally murdered, she lost her mind completely. In those days, most people, including pirates, believed that if you harmed someone who was mentally ill, the wrath of God would descend on you. Thus the pirates took Theodosia ashore with them and cared for her.

The story goes on to say that from that time on Theodosia would walk the beach all day long, sometimes with her portrait in her arms, and say to anyone around, "I'm going home to New York to see my father." She lived this way on Hatteras for many years and grew to be very old. On a rainy day in 1869, as she lay dying, she was attended by Dr. William G. Poole of Elizabeth City, North Carolina. Dr. Poole often made the trip out to the islands to attend to the "bankers'" needs. Most of the pirates had long since died and the people on the island had no idea who Theodosia was. Dr. Poole was loved by these folks, who were very grateful for his many trips to take care of them at no cost.

While the doctor was with Theodosia Alston on that day, the gentle rain slowly intensified and became a "nor' easter." As the fury of the storm slammed into the island, Dr. Poole and those inside Theodosia's shack huddled together to ride it out. Looking at the portrait that hung on the wall, Dr. Poole asked, "Who is that in the portrait and where did it come from?" The islanders said they didn't know and they really didn't know who the "touched" woman in the shack was, either. She had been there longer than any of them could remember. Then one of the islanders said, "Doctor, you been so kind to us, we know that if this here woman was in her right mind she'd gladly give you the portrait as payment." The man then got up and removed the portrait from the wall.

As he did, Theodosia jumped up from her bed and screamed, "No, that's mine! I'm going home to New York to see my father!" Then Theodosia grabbed the portrait from the islander and ran out into the storm to meet the rushing embrace of the ocean's surf. Her body was never found, but the portrait was later discovered on the beach. The islanders did give the portrait to Dr. Poole. He kept it in his Elizabeth City home until his death some years later.

Theodosia Alston's story doesn't end with that storm on Hatteras. There were many searches made for her by the United States Navy, her husband, Joseph Alston, and her father, but no trace of Theodosia or the *Patriot* was ever found until Dr. Poole's discovery of the portrait. By then, both Aaron Burr and Joseph Alston had been dead for decades. Aaron Burr died in New York in 1836 and Joseph Alston died in South Carolina in 1816, just four years after his wife's disappearance. He was buried at his plantation in Murrell's Inlet. A monument there is dedicated to him and speaks of "those whose loss had left in his heart an aching void that nothing on earth could fill."

Legends of Theodosia Alston still haunt us. Whether she was made to walk the plank by pirates, was the crazy woman of Hatteras Island, or was just lost at sea with everyone else aboard the *Patriot,* no one will ever know. Regardless of which version of the story is true, the ironic twist is that Theodosia Burr Alston, the only child of Aaron Burr, the man who killed Alexander Hamilton, disappeared within sight of the Hamilton Light!

Theodosia Alston's portrait hung in the Macbeth Art Gallery in New York City for years, but its current whereabouts, like Theodosia's fate, is a mystery.

Jules Bledsoe

The Voice

The two things that Jules Bledsoe always wanted to do were to make sick people well and to sing. As a child he sang to himself and in church. The people who heard him knew that there was something special about this child. Throughout his early life, his one ambition was to be a doctor. But Jules was born with a gift: his voice. And that voice yearned to be heard. As time went on that voice became an incredible mix of purity, soul, and heart.

Born in Waco, Texas, on December 29, 1898, to two former slaves, Jules Bledsoe yearned for an education, because he knew he needed one to become a doctor. But he also worked hard to help support his family. While he toiled, Bledsoe sang for his own enjoyment. This went on for several years until he studied medicine at Columbia University in New York. His love for medicine was only surpassed by his love of music, and he began taking voice and music lessons between his other classes.

Soon Bledsoe began appearing in local concerts. He was successful, and gave up his medical studies to pursue his music career full time. In 1924, Jules Bledsoe made his concert debut as a baritone at

Aeolian Hall in New York. After two more years of concentrated study and performing, Bledsoe made his stage debut as Tizah in Frank Harding's opera "Deep River."

One year later, the great composer Jerome Kern heard Bledsoe's incredible, now bass, voice. Kern had been working on Edna Ferber's novel *Show Boat* as a musical. After hearing Bledsoe, Kern created the part of "Joe" for him and wrote the song "Old Man River" for Bledsoe's voice. Bledsoe was personally selected by Kern to star in Florence Ziegfield's production of "Show Boat," but unfortunately Paul Robeson, who soon came to personify the role, was chosen for the British premiere. Robeson was also picked to play the role of "Joe" in the first motion picture version of *Show Boat*. This disappointment did not deter Bledsoe. He had his eye on other things. In 1925 he was appointed to the music staff at the Roxy Theater on Broadway, the first African American artist to be continuously employed by a Broadway theater.

In 1934 Bledsoe sang the title role in a European tour of Gruenberg's opera "Emperor Jones." Again, Paul Robeson was selected to star in this role for the motion picture of the same name. (This role was originally created for a white man, Lawrence Tibbett, in the Metropolitan Opera in New York.)

Jules Bledsoe continued breaking color barriers with his voice and was the first African American to sing in the Metropolitan Opera House. He continued to star in smaller opera companies and in 1933 did a series, "Songs of the Negro," for the British Broadcasting Company. In 1936 he starred in "Blackbirds of 1936."

Jules Bledsoe died on July 14, 1943, in Hollywood, California. He was not making a movie. He had just completed a concert tour for American servicemen. Luckily, there are still recordings available of this man's incredible voice. Although few people even know who Jules Bledsoe was, his impact on music was to help bring down the color barriers when Broadway and the movies did not use African American performers.

Charles Gates Dawes

He Won the Nobel Peace Prize and Wrote a Song That Went to the Top 40

He was a brilliant businessman, an incredibly gifted musician and composer, a soldier who stood up to Congress, and a politician who hated politics (and the president of the United States for whom he served as vice-president). And he was the man who came up with the idea that finally put Chicago's gangster Al Capone in jail. His name was Charles Gates Dawes.

Dawes was born in the last year of the Civil War in Marietta, Ohio. For the first ten years of his life, he watched life in his home town with the curious eyes of a child. He listened to many of the veterans of that great war as they told their stories and he watched as the town around him grew during the Reconstruction years.

By the time Dawes was eleven, President U. S. Grant had established the first national park in the United States: Yellowstone, while in that same year George Armstrong Custer died at the Little Bighorn in Montana. The United States was growing by leaps and bounds through its movement west.

By the time Dawes was nineteen, he had already obtained a degree in engineering from Marietta College. Two years later he received his law degree from the University of Cincinnati. He was admitted to the bar in 1886 and set up a law practice in Lincoln, Nebraska. Later, Dawes moved to Chicago, where he was extremely successful with his law practice until 1897. His reputation as an honest lawyer and a man of conviction helped him to win an appointment by President William McKinley as comptroller of the currency. Dawes was only thirty-two years old. By 1901, with his term in office over, Dawes moved back to Chicago and founded the Central Trust Company of Illinois, where, for the next sixteen years, he prospered.

In 1917, World War I brought Dawes into the United States Army. He was commissioned as a major in the prestigious Engineering Corps and quickly rose to the rank of brigadier general. He was later transferred, because of his success in finance, to be the purchasing agent for the American Expeditionary Forces under General John J. Pershing.

When the war ended, Dawes made national headlines because of his testimony to a congressional committee investigating charges of overpayment for military supplies. Never one to mince words with anyone, Dawes subjected the congressmen questioning his honesty to a verbal barrage: "Sure we paid. We didn't dicker. ... We would have paid horse prices for sheep if sheep could have pulled artillery to the front. ... Hell and Maria, we weren't trying to keep a set of books, we were trying to win the war!" From that time on Charles Gates Dawes was nicknamed "Hell and Maria Dawes."

Dawes was one of the very first private citizens to take on Congress, and his honesty won the hearts of the American people. In 1922 President Warren G. Harding appointed Dawes the nation's first director of the Budget Bureau. In 1924, as chairman of the reparations committee examining the financial conditions in Germany, he devised the Dawes Plan, reducing reparations payments and otherwise stabilizing the German economy. For this plan he was awarded the 1925 Nobel Peace Prize.

In 1925, after President Harding died, Vice-President Calvin Coolidge took office as the president. Charles Gates Dawes was appointed vice-president. The problem with this arrangement was that

Dawes disliked Coolidge intensely. In fact, Dawes sent a letter to President Coolidge telling him that he did not wish to attend any cabinet meetings. To add injury to insult, on Inauguration Day, Dawes stole the national spotlight from the president by taking the occasion to denounce the Congress of the United States. The straw that broke the camel's back, though, was when one of Coolidge's nominees for attorney general failed to get confirmation by a tie vote. Dawes, as presiding officer of the Senate, could have broken the tie in the administration's favor, but was nowhere on the Senate floor. He was napping at Willard Hotel.

It was during Dawes's tenure as vice-president, in the time of Prohibition, that Al Capone ruled the streets of Chicago. Capone and his mob controlled the sales and distribution of illegal liquor. Mob wars ravaged the streets with drive-by shootings in which both gangsters and civilians died in the crossfire of machine gun bullets. The local police departments of Chicago and its suburbs were bought and paid for by Capone and other gangsters. The FBI couldn't come up with any evidence to convict Capone on any of the murders for which he and his gang were responsible. It was Dawes who came up with the idea that finally put Al Capone away. Dawes, as a businessman, figured that there was a good chance Capone wasn't paying any taxes on the money he earned. He conferred with the Internal Revenue Service about the possibility of Capone being an income tax evader. After a lengthy investigation, the IRS found proof that the gangster had indeed not paid any income taxes on his illegal businesses. It was this avenue of law enforcement that finally put the infamous gangster in prison.

After Dawes left office, he served as an ambassador to Great Britain and then under President Herbert Hoover as president of the Reconstruction Finance Corporation.

Throughout his political career, Dawes always made time for one of his great passions: music. Dawes was an accomplished musician and composer. His favorite instrument was the violin. In 1911, although busy with his financial affairs, Charles Gates Dawes took the time to compose a piece for violin called "Melody in A Major." It achieved some success in the 1920s, but it became a number one hit in 1957, during the golden era of rock and roll, when words were added to that melody. The name of the song was "It's All in the Game," and it was recorded by Tommy Edwards.

Charles Gates Dawes did not live to hear his song on the radio. He died in 1951.

Ten Interesting Facts
about Presidents and Vice-Presidents

1. Thomas Riley Marshall, vice-president under President Woodrow Wilson, once got bored while listening to a speech by Senator Joseph L. Bristow of Kansas. The senator droned on for over an hour about "what this country needs." Sitting in his perch as presiding officer, Marshall interjected, "What this country needs is a good five cent cigar!" When asked about the significance of the office of vice-president, Marshall replied, "Once there were two brothers. One ran away to sea, the other was elected vice president, and nothing was ever heard of either of them again."

Unlike Dawes, Marshall was extremely loyal to and fond of the president for whom he worked. When Wilson had a stroke in 1919, Marshall refused to take over as acting president.

2. Richard Nixon was the first vice-president to be born in the twentieth century. When he ran for president in 1960, his opponent was John F. Kennedy. Kennedy won and became the first president of the United States to be born in the twentieth century.

3. William Howard Taft was the heaviest president in our history. He weighed in at 323 pounds while in the White House and was the only president who, because of his weight, got stuck in the White House bathtub!

After Taft finished his term as president, he taught at Yale University. In 1921, President Warren G. Harding appointed Taft Chief Justice of the United States. William Howard Taft was the only man in history to serve as the head of both the executive and judicial branches of the U.S. government.

4. President William Henry Harrison gave the longest inaugural speech in history and served the shortest term of any president. He caught a cold, which later turned to pneumonia. He died thirty days after taking office. He was the first president to die in office. Harrison's grandson Benjamin Harrison was elected as the 23rd president of the United States in 1888. As do all presidents, he won the election through the electoral college. Had the election been based on the popular vote, he would have lost to his opponent, Grover Cleveland, by 100,476 votes.

5. Theodore Roosevelt was the youngest man ever sworn in as president of the United States, after the assassination of President William McKinley in 1901. He was forty-two years old. John F. Kennedy was the youngest man ever elected president of the United States. He was forty-three.

6. President Martin Van Buren's vice-president, Richard Mentor Johnson, had taken a slave woman as his common-law wife and raised and educated their mulatto children as free persons. This made him an extremely unpopular man in the South. Johnson was himself a Southerner. There were three vice-presidents named Johnson: Richard Mentor Johnson, Andrew Johnson, and Lyndon B. Johnson. All three were Southerners, but only Andrew and Lyndon became presidents. Andrew Johnson became president after Abraham Lincoln was assassinated and Lyndon Johnson became president after John F. Kennedy was killed in Dallas in 1963.

7. At thirty-six, Vice-President of the United States John Cabell Breckinridge, who served under President James Buchanan, was the youngest man ever to serve in that position. When his term was over in 1861 and the Civil War broke out, Breckinridge left the Union and became a major general in the Confederate Army. On February 6, 1865, just two months before the war ended, he was appointed Secretary of War for the Confederate States of America.

8. The first assassination attempt on a U.S. president occurred on January 30, 1835. As President Andrew Jackson was leaving the Capitol, a thirty-two-year-old mentally disturbed man named Richard Lawrence walked up to within about thirteen feet of Jackson and fired a single-shot derringer. The percussion cap exploded but did not discharge the powder. This act infuriated Jackson, who then tried to strike the would-be assassin with his cane. Now at point blank range, Lawrence fired a second derringer at Jackson. It too failed to fire. The odds against this happening were put at one in 125,000. Lawrence was found not guilty by reason of insanity at his trial, but was put in a mental institution until his death in 1861.

Jackson was also the first president to be photographed and the only president who paid off the national debt. He was also the only president who disobeyed the Supreme Court of the United States. When the Court told him that depriving the Cherokee Nation of their lands was unconstitutional, Jackson had the United States Army forcibly remove the Cherokee to "Indian Territory" (present-day Oklahoma). Thousands of Cherokee died from hunger and exhaustion. This journey was known as "The Trail of Tears." The irony of this story is that Jackson's adopted son was a Cherokee.

9. President Grover Cleveland was a "draft dodger." After being drafted during the Civil War, Cleveland chose to purchase a substitute, a legal option under the terms of the Conscription Act of 1863. He paid $150 to a thirty-two-year-old Polish immigrant to serve in his place. At age forty-nine, Cleveland married twenty-one-year-old Frances Folsom in the White House. He was the only president to be married there. He had met his bride shortly after she was born. He was a good friend of her father, Oscar Folsom. Cleveland served two terms as president, but they were not consecutive. He was defeated by Benjamin Harrison during his bid for re-election. Four years later, he defeated Benjamin Harrison during Harrison's bid for re-election.

10. The only two signers of the Declaration of Independence to become president were John Adams (the second president of the United States) and Thomas Jefferson (the third president of the United States). By a weird coincidence, these two men died on the same day exactly fifty years after they had signed that document: July 4, 1826.

The Day Doris Miller Became a Man

Prior to World War II, the U.S. military, by law, prohibited any African American from being a combatant or picking up and firing any kind of firearm. African Americans were only allowed to be cooks or stewards and were commonly called "boy." When the Japanese bombed Pearl Harbor on December 7, 1941, Doris Miller, who was a cook aboard the battleship USS *West Virginia,* disobeyed a direct order from his captain and broke a federal law by becoming the first African American to fight against an enemy in World War II.

The *West Virginia*'s captain lay on the quarterdeck severely wounded and ordered Miller and others to abandon ship. Miller refused to obey the order, moved his captain to safety, ran over to a 50-caliber machine gun, pulled the dead gunner's mate off the gun, and proceeded to shoot down five Japanese Zeros that morning. On that day Doris Miller was no longer a "boy"; he'd become a man in the eyes of those who witnessed his heroics. Miller's story is told in a poem.

Dorrie Miller was a man in the time of World War Two.
And he went down in history as a hero through and through.
He was born near old Waco and he was born both poor and black.
His daddy was a sharecropper whose work could break your back.

In the year of thirty-nine, when he left his Texas home,
Dorrie joined the U. S. Navy to see the world and roam.
He was sent to Hawaii aboard a ship to serve
And on that fateful Sunday morn, Dorrie never lost his nerve.

It was Sunday, December seventh in the year of forty-one,
When Dorrie's cooking was shattered by a bomb and the sounds of guns.
He ran up for the quarter deck in his commissary whites,
And Dorrie became the first black man to take up his country's fight.

Well they threw all they had at us to bring us to our knees,
When Pearl Harbor was attacked that day by the Japanese.
And of all the men who fought that day his deeds alone still stand,
For in that time of World War Two, Dorrie Miller was a man.

Well the Captain he was wounded and the gunner's mate was dead.
And in the Hell that followed Dorrie filled the sky with lead.
He shot down his first zero, then two, then three, then four,
And before that day was over, Dorrie shot down just one more.

Yes, they threw all they had at us to bring us to our knees,
When Pearl Harbor was attacked that day by the Japanese.
And of all the men who fought that day, his deeds alone still stand.
For in that time of World War Two, Dorrie Miller was a man.

Doris "Dorrie" Miller was given the Navy's highest award for valor, the Navy Cross. He was not given the Congressional Medal of Honor because he was black. In 1942, "Dorrie" was assigned as a cook aboard a destroyer in the South Pacific. His ship was torpedoed by a Japanese submarine. He did not survive. Some years later the Navy named a ship in his honor: USS *Doris Miller.* Ships named after Navy Cross recipients are in the destroyer class, that is, destroyers, destroyer escorts, or frigates. These are the smallest and fastest of U.S. naval fighting ships.

The First Shots Fired on December 7, 1941

The first shots fired on the morning of December 7, 1941, were from an American destroyer. A small American minesweep (a naval ship made of wood, designed to detect and remove floating magnetic mines) signaled the USS *Ward,* a World War I-era destroyer, that it had spotted the conning tower of a submarine. Within moments, the *Ward*'s crew had sighted the green-colored conning tower of a Japanese two-man midget submarine trailing behind an American supply ship.

The *Ward*'s skipper, Lieutenant William W. Outerbridge, called his crew to general quarters (battle stations) and commenced firing on the Japanese sub. At 6:45 in the morning the destroyer opened fire. A shell from the ship's number 3 gun hit the sub's conning tower, causing the sub to spin out of control. The sub then sank below the waters of the Pacific, killing the two Japanese sailors aboard, making them the first two casualties of December 7, 1941.

Billie and Patches

S he was a Cherokee woman who came to Colorado from Oklahoma in the 1920s. Her grandfather was a chief who survived the "Trail of Tears." You won't read about her in a history book, but once in awhile you might see an article about her in one of Denver's newspapers. Billie Preston is not rich or famous. Some people thought she was crazy, but to others she was an everyday hero, and she still is to those who know her.

Throughout Billie's life, her only mode of transportation has been a horse. In earlier years, she could be seen riding through the streets of Aurora, Colorado, on a daily basis. Many times she stopped at a business and asked them to donate toys. When they did she tied them to her saddle and took them home. Around Christmas time, Billie would call up a business that had a large truck and ask them to come to her house to pick up all of the toys she'd collected. When the truck arrived, Billie asked them to load up all of the toys and transport them to the State Home, Colorado's state orphanage. Billie wanted to make sure all the children there got something for Christmas.

Over the years, the state of Colorado abandoned its orphanage system for foster home care, so Billie could no longer continue her toy-collecting activities. Then the city of Aurora did something that almost cost Billie her horse Patches.

When the city of Aurora annexed the land where Billie lived, a city ordinance was enacted that plainly stated, "There shall be no livestock permitted in the City of Aurora." When Billie's new neighbors saw her small corral and her horse Patches, they called the city to complain. The police came out and issued Billie a citation ordering her into court to explain why she had a horse in the city.

To make a long story short, Billie was asked if she were guilty or not of having brought a horse into the city and she replied, "No. The city is guilty of bringing itself out to me and my horse. We were here long before the city was." The judge eventually agreed with Billie and told her that she could keep Patches until he died, but after that she would not be allowed to have another horse. That was in 1956. Patches died in 1969. So I guess you could say that the city of Aurora, Colorado, was officially a "one horse" town from 1956 to 1969.

Billie's story doesn't end there, though. A few years ago, after recovering from an accident that blinded her (she dropped a bottle of ammonia into a bucket of bleach), Billie told the city that she would deed over some of her land if they built a recreation center for the children in the neighborhood. They agreed, and from that time until recently Billie had been a regular visitor there. The folks who work in the recreation center used to go over to Billie's house, just across the street, to make sure that she was all right. They would then bring her over to the recreation center to visit with the kids. Before she told any stories, though, Billie would say, "No coffee, no talky." After her coffee, she'd tell anyone who would listen what life was like seventy years ago, when what is now city was all prairie.

The prairie and Billie are both gone from this location. In her mid-nineties Billie finally got to the point where she couldn't be alone anymore. Her frail health forced her into a nursing home, but her spirit remains strong.

In her Cherokee veins there's the blood of Chiefs,
That rode the "Trail of Tears."
Her hair is white and her voice is soft,
'Cause Billie's getting on in years.

She likes to talk of days gone by
When she lit her smokes with matches,
And if you look beyond her now blind eyes
They light up when you talk about Patches.

Billie and Patches rode the streets of town,
Carrying a gift called love.
And they took it to the young and spread it all around,
For a new kind of world to dream of.
Yeah, they took it all around and spread it up and down
For a new kind of world to dream of.

Patches was a horse that she rode alone
To a hundred streets and places.
Collecting toys for homeless girls and boys,
To bring some joy to their faces.

But, those times and deeds are now long gone,
And so's a horse she named Patches.
And in a house she built, she still lives on,
Bringing joy to those she still touches.

Billie and Patches rode the streets of town,
Carrying a gift called love.
And they took it to the young and spread it all around,
For a new kind of world to dream of.
Yeah, they took it all around and spread it up and down
For a new kind of world to dream of.

12

Sam Antonio

The Last Acoma to Survive

When Sam Antonio left home for the United States Army, he never dreamed that he would become one of the "Battling Bastards of Bataan." Nor would he have ever dreamed that he would spend three and a half years in a Japanese prisoner of war camp in Manchuria. He didn't think of these things because his mother had told him that he and his three brothers would all come back from the war alive. At the time she made the prediction the United States was not involved in war, so this was odd. Sam's mother blessed Sam before he left for basic training. This was not an unusual thing for Sam's mother to do; everyone in the Pueblo knew that she was a powerful medicine woman. She had cured many of her own people of illnesses white doctors said were terminal and on occasion she could see into the future. And she had seen a war coming.

Sam Antonio and five other Acoma (pronounced Ah Kah Mah) boys had been inducted into the army in that spring of 1940. In August 1941, they were sent to the Philippine Islands as part of the 200th Coastal Artillery Unit from New Mexico. Army life and the Philippines were totally foreign to Sam Antonio's Acoma way of life.

The marching, hiking, and food in cans were not part of his culture, for when Sam Antonio was a little boy, "fast food" meant a rabbit.

And being able to run a rabbit down took a great deal of speed and agility on his part. Not only would he chase after the rabbit, but from the late spring to early fall, he also dodged the many rattlesnakes that made their homes in the desert. If Sam Antonio failed to catch a rabbit or two, it would mean a meatless meal or hunger for everyone in his household. He and his dog Hickquay rarely failed. They had the art of rabbit hunting down so precisely that Hickquay would find a rabbit and chase it towards Sam. Sam in turn had a long stick with notches carved on the tip. If the rabbit made its way past Sam and into a hole or behind the rocks at the base of the mesa, he was able to take the stick and reach into the hole or behind the rocks and twist it into the rabbit's fur to pull it out. Yes, Sam Antonio was fast and he grew up following the ancient ways of his Acoma people.

Sam grew up not far from Grants, New Mexico, near the ancient Acoma Pueblo, known as Sky City. It is the oldest pueblo in the United States where people have lived continuously for over 600 years. Within sight of this pueblo is the Enchanted Mesa, which was the first place the Acoma had located their village. The Acoma say that they once lived high on that rock, while down below they farmed in the fertile grasslands. There was only one way up to the village, a very steep incline. One day there was either a terrible earthquake or a thunderstorm that destroyed the pathway to the village. It was said that those on top of the rock starved to death and those who were down below created Sky City. This story had been handed down through the centuries. From this and other stories, Sam Antonio learned how his people prayed to the dawning sun and the setting sun each day. He spoke only his native tongue of Acoma until he was seven years old. That was when the county sheriff came.

Sam Antonio and others had reached school age, and Bureau of Indian Affairs (BIA) regulations stated that all children of school age would be taken from their homes (sometimes forcibly) and sent to an Indian boarding school. Sam was sent to Santa Fe, New Mexico. For the next few years he lived and went to school in Santa Fe. He was allowed home visits only on holidays and summer breaks. Boarding school did all it could to take the "Indian" out of Sam Antonio and the others who were there. They were taught English and how to read and write, but were punished if they spoke their own language or worshipped in their own religion. In 1936, however, Sam was allowed to go back to his home, where he was one of the first Native Americans to attend public high school in Grants, New Mexico. His natural ability for sports allowed him to excel in all that he tried: baseball, basketball, football, and track. Because of his early training in chasing down rabbits, Sam Antonio became one of the fastest 880-yard runners in New Mexico, but it was his boxing ability that won him an AAU National Championship in 1939 in the 118-pound featherweight division.

After he graduated from high school, Sam Antonio went to work for the railroad in Grants. One day he saw a familiar face in the railyards. It was a Lakota friend of his whom he knew from his days in boarding school. They talked for awhile, then the friend asked Sam what he was doing there. Sam explained that he was working for the railroad. His friend laughed and said that he was riding the rails. He was a hobo. "Sam," he said, "Why don't you come ride the rails with me? It's great adventure and I'll teach you all you need to know."

It sounded good to Sam, and without hesitation he and his friend caught the next train out of Grants for points unknown. Sam said no good-byes to anyone, he just left New Mexico on the hobo trail. For weeks he traveled with people of all races who lived the hobo life. At each stop they all had two important jobs: don't get caught by the "bulls" (the law) and scrounge up some food to share with everyone in camp. When the opportunity presented itself, Sam Antonio would catch a rabbit. Sam didn't know it at the time, but some of this training would help save his life two years later.

As the weeks went by, Sam finally got homesick and decided to go back to New Mexico. All the time he was gone, his family didn't know whether he was alive or dead. When he arrived home, his angry but thankful mother asked him where he'd been. After he told her his story she asked, "Why didn't you write?" Without hesitation Sam answered, "Because I knew you didn't know how to read." When she realized what Sam had said was true, she laughed, but added, "But your sister could have read it to me."

Then the time came when Sam Antonio was finally inducted into the United States Army, in the spring of 1940. As a matter of fact, it was April Fool's day. He thought it was a joke at first, but then realized it wasn't when four days later he and five other Acoma boys were sent to Fort Bliss, Texas for basic training.

When basic training was over, Sam and the others stayed on at Fort Bliss for artillery training. They became part of the 200th Coastal Artillery Unit from New Mexico and were shipped off to the Philippine Islands in August 1941.

In the Philippines, Sam found islands beautiful with lush jungles and exotic plants and birds. And coming from the deserts of New Mexico, the crystal clear Pacific waters were an incredible sight. Mangos were ripe, as were coconuts and bananas. But the poverty and simple lifestyle of the friendly Filipino people, amid the world of whites, reminded Sam Antonio of his own people. Within four months, however, all this would change and the Philippines, the world, and Sam's life would never be the same again.

On December 8, 1941, the day after Pearl Harbor, Sam and the other soldiers first heard the planes outside of their billeted area near Clark Field, not far from Manila. They ran outside to see who was flying over. The planes were flying too high to identify, but one of the men in Sam's group counted fifty-four. At first they all thought the planes were U.S. naval flyers, but then the first bombs began falling around them and onto Clark Field. High-level Japanese bombers caught the United States Army Air Corps forces on the ground. Eighteen of thirty-five B-17 bombers and fifty-six fighters were destroyed in the initial attack. Sam Antonio and the others were horrified. They had heard the news about Pearl Harbor, but they didn't expect the war to reach them so quickly and with such devastation. The next day the United States Navy pulled its Asiatic Fleet out of the Philippines and the remaining B-17s flew south to Australia. Small Japanese parties began landing on the Philippine Islands. Starting on the 22nd and 23rd of December the main invasion groups landed.

General Douglas MacArthur ordered all military units to retreat to the Bataan Peninsula. They accomplished this in a leap-frog manner.

One unit would protect another's retreat and they would in turn be pro-tected by another. The inexperienced troops executed this maneuver brilliantly until the 80,000 men and their artillery gained the peninsula on January 6, 1942.

Greatly outgunned, U.S. troops and Filipino scouts began to dig in for the coming onslaught and began plans for guerrilla warfare.

Armed with Springfield 30.06 rifles that were made in 1903 and World War I and older artillery, Sam Antonio and the other defenders were no match for the huge Japanese army and their modern weapons. But they used what they had effectively during the next five months before Bataan fell. From December 1941 until his surrender in May 1942, Sam Antonio witnessed incredible feats of heroism. On more than one occasion he saw Filipino cavalry chasing Japanese tanks with their horses. If they could get up along side of the tank, they would pull the pin of a grenade and try to toss it into the tank's hatch. On more than one occasion they succeeded. Some of those men lived to tell about it. For those who did not, Sam tells their story for them.

Sam Antonio and others fought in the immense jungles of the Philippines day after day, waiting for what General Douglas MacArthur had promised in his letter of January 15, 1942:

> Help is on the way from the United States. Thousands of troops and hundreds of planes are being dispatched. The exact time of arrival of reinforcements is unknown as they will have to fight their way through Japanese against them. It is imperative that our troops hold until these reinforcements arrive. No further retreat is possible. ... I call upon every soldier in Bataan to fight in his assigned position, resisting every attack. This is the only road to salvation.

MacArthur's words were inspiring, but everyone knew that if help did not arrive soon it would only be a matter of time before they were overrun by the Japanese. But there was no help. The Pacific Fleet had been destroyed. American and Filipino military forces in the Philippines were greatly outgunned, though not outmanned. For the next three months they gave ground, but they made the Japanese pay for it in blood. Over the following two months, they took everything the Imperial Japanese Army threw at them, but finally, on April 8, 1941, Bataan fell. On the next day most of its defenders surrendered. They were out of food and almost totally out of ammunition.

Sam Antonio and the other survivors waited by the beach at Mariveles, on the southern tip of the peninsula. One of the men in Sam's unit saw a boat out on the water. If he and others could reach it they might be able to make it to Corregidor. Sam and seven others made the trip on two boats. One of the boats was a small craft that Sam had scrounged. To the south of them, across about three miles of open ocean, lay the island of Corregidor. The Americans, now under the command of General Jonathan Wainwright (General MacArthur had been ordered out of the Philippines by President Roosevelt.) still held the island.

Sam Antonio and the others were the lucky ones. Day turned into night as they paddled for over nine hours in shark-infested waters. They finally made it to Corregidor and successfully avoided the Japanese troops that had already landed on that island. Those who could not make it off Bataan were forced to surrender on that day.

After surrendering, some 75,000 U.S. soldiers and Filipino scouts were force marched from Mariveles, in the south, to a railroad siding at San Fernando, forty miles away. Many of these men had already come down with malaria and dysentery from lack of proper food and medical attention. The infamous death march had begun.

The Japanese denied these men all food and water under the blinding tropical sun, and if a prisoner fell down from exhaustion, he was either shot or bayoneted. If a prisoner spoke out, he was viciously beaten or killed. Once in awhile a Japanese office would test how sharp his samurai sword was by randomly cutting off the head of a prisoner who was straggling from formation. Between 7,000 and 10,000 men died, 2,300 of them Americans, on this march to the first of many POW (prisoner of war) camps. Sam Antonio was not one of them.

Through courage seldom seen in the face of such overwhelming odds, Sam and the others had proudly earned their nickname: "The

Battling Bastards of Bataan." Those who did not get off Bataan that day were now at the mercy of their captors, who, just a couple of years earlier, had murdered thousands of Manchurian civilians.

Sam Antonio and those who made it to Corregidor would only know freedom for twenty-seven days. On May 6, 1942, General Jonathan Wainwright surrendered to an overwhelming enemy. Sam was taken prisoner. Although he would try time and again, there would be no escape.

A new roundup of prisoners began after General Wainwright surrendered his forces. Many of the men had hoped for some decent food, for they had been eating snakes, monkeys, and iguanas for the past couple of months. The running joke was that the GIs had made all of the snakes and iguanas extinct species on Bataan and Corregidor. But decent food and care did not come. After Sam Antonio and the others were herded together, the commander of the Imperial Japanese Army in the Philippines, General Homa, came to the great tunnel fortress of Corregidor to take Wainwright's formal surrender. All of the prisoners were ordered to observe the ceremony and salute or bow down to General Homa and the flag of Japan. But Sam and a friend, Jose Isidro Cata, a Pueblo Indian from the San Juan Pueblo in New Mexico, slipped away and hid underneath a truck that had been destroyed during the fighting.

There beneath that truck, avoiding the hot tropical sun, Sam Antonio made a vow that he would not bow down or salute that flag. For although in his Acoma ways Sam had always prayed to the morning sunrise, he'd be damned if he would bow or salute to the flag of the "rising sun." Sam was not caught that day, but he had nowhere to escape to, so he rejoined the main body of his unit. Then the looting started.

Japanese guards began moving through the ranks and taking anything of value from the prisoners: rings, watches, necklaces, and wallets. If a prisoner refused he was severely beaten or killed. The Japanese used pillowcases to hold their loot.

Then the Japanese began to separate Americans and Filipino scouts. Sam and others from his unit and others were separated and taken to the coast. They were to be shipped away from the Philippines to points unknown. They didn't know if they were going to be killed. They were taken from Corregidor, by ship, back to Bataan, and unloaded. On their march to Manila, Sam and the others were amazed at the greetings that came from the Filipino people. The people were astounded that Sam and the other Americans were still alive. From the side of the roads, the gathering Filipinos threw out cigarettes, candy, bananas, rice balls, and money. Americans who fell from exhaustion were helped to their feet by the Filipinos. The Japanese did not interfere. The crowds thinned out as Sam and the others continued to march to a prison camp called Bilibid. For the next few weeks conditions were horrible. It got worse when they were sent to another prison camp called Cabanatuan.

The Americans were marched from Bilibid to a railyard and literally crammed into box and cattle cars like sardines without the oil. The smell of sweat and human waste was to become common. Fights broke out for space in the cramped cars and two more Americans died. The Japanese told the prisoners that if any more trouble broke out they would kill ten men. The prisoners tried to get any comfort they could find as they traveled to Cabanatuan.

Sam Antonio and the other prisoners were taken off the train and marched a short distance to the Cabanatuan schoolyard. It had been converted into a temporary prison. They were given food and water and rest. On the next day they would start a twelve-mile march. The march took hours in the fly-infested heat. Again stragglers were beaten and prodded with bayonets until they finally reached their destination. The only good thing to greet Sam was the other five Acomas who had been in his unit. All six men had survived up to that point.

From July until October the Americans lived in extremely primitive conditions. They had no bathrooms. What they did have was a long ditch in which water ran through the camp. It was called a "straddle-sleuth." If a man had to relieve himself, he would straddle the ditch to do so. Many men were so weak that when the attempted this they would fall in. Some died there. In October, word had gone out that a select few men (about a thousand men) were to be shipped out of

Cabanatuan to Manila. They were going to be sent out of the Philippines. Sam Antonio was among those chosen.

They were told they were going to be marched to Manila. But something was very different in the way that they were treated on this march to the coast. They weren't beaten, shot, stabbed, or abused in any way. And their march was not a forced one, as had been the case only months before. Once they reached Manila they were taken to Pier 7, where pots of steamed rice awaited them. Food! Food was always on their minds. Food and escape took over their thoughts. Sam Antonio and the others waited for two days before they were met by another group of American prisoners from another camp. There were about 2,000 men awaiting the Japanese freighter *Hokka Maru.* They were told that they were going to Manchuria. They were to be workers in the machine shops and mills there to support the Japanese war machine.

Once the ship arrived, the prisoners were put below decks. Again, there was not enough room for everyone. And again there were no bathroom facilities aboard this ship. After the first few hours at sea, the lower decks were covered with feces, urine, and vomit and there was no fresh air. Some men went up to the main deck of the ship, preferring the risk of death to the squalor below. Sam Antonio was confined below. While he was down there the *Hokka Maru* became the target of an American or British submarine. Two torpedoes were fired at the ship full of prisoners, but Fate intervened. Miraculously, this big clumsy ship was able to outmaneuver the sub's torpedoes and continued on to Formosa.

The sanitation conditions did not improve until the Japanese soldiers themselves started complaining about how bad the smells below were. Those who died in these wretched conditions were buried at sea. Fire hoses were finally brought down and the Japanese began spraying the men and their quarters alike.

After the *Hokka Maru* reached port in Formosa, the men were transferred to a newer freighter called the *Hokka Maru 2.* From there they sailed until they reached Fusan port in Korea. Sam Antonio and the others were then sent by rail to Manchuria. The name of their prison camp was Mukden. For the next three and a half years, Sam was sent to work in the textile shop, making canvas in the fall and winter. But in the spring and summer months, Sam was put to work in the fields as a farmer. He and the others planted a variety of food for the rest of the prisoners and the guards. This was a detail that Sam enjoyed because he got to eat when he wasn't supposed to. Carrots! He ate a lot of carrots to help keep away the ever-present pangs of hunger!

Throughout his three and a half years in Mukden, Sam Antonio continually tried to escape. During one attempt he accidentally came in contact with an electric fence. The force of the electricity threw him back to the ground violently. The man with him had to revive him. The burns he received were so severe that he burned off his fingerprints. (To this day he jokes about how he could go out and commit a crime and get away with it. The reason for it, he laughs, is that the police would never be able to identify him through his fingerprints, because he doesn't have any.) Sam and many other Americans at Mukden continually sabotaged the machines on which they worked. Most of the machines were American made, and if they could put the equipment out of commission, the Japanese had no way of replacing broken parts.

Finally, in August 1945, Sam and the other prisoners at Mukden knew something was happening. They could see and hear American airplanes flying overhead and there was almost no resistance from the Japanese. Once when the bombers came in to bomb the factories, one of the bombs went astray and landed in an American barracks. Nineteen U.S. prisoners were killed.

Shortly thereafter, members of the OSS (the forerunner to today's CIA) parachuted into the prison grounds, to the shock of everyone there. They had come to tell the Japanese that the war was over. Two atomic bombs had been dropped on Japan itself. At first these Americans were not believed, but the Japanese knew that the Soviets were fast approaching Mukden. Within days they arrived and liberated the camp. Sam Antonio couldn't believe his eyes. Within the ranks of the Soviet troops were women. Some of them were officers and others were noncoms. They had fought with the men through China and had come to liberate Mukden.

Real food came in by the truckload and the men who had been prisoners now watched as their captors were disarmed and imprisoned. Of the six Acoma who went to Bataan, only three remained alive. In the following years, one died not long after the war and in 1995, Tom Charlie, the only other Acoma to survive, died in New Mexico.

Now Sam Antonio is the only Acoma survivor of those terrible years. He came home and married and he also chose to stay in the military for the next twelve years. In 1947, Sam obtained his pilot's license, flying single-engine aircraft. His adventures in the sky would fill a volume of books, but that is another story.

In 1958, Sam left the military and went to work as a uranium miner, literally next to the land in which he was born. After a very short stint underground, Sam became a mechanic with the mining company and stayed above the ground for the next sixteen years. Sam Antonio is now retired, but keeps up the pace of a man much younger than his seventy-eight years. In the summer of 1996 Sam had both knees replaced and today he continues to hunt and drive all over his beloved New Mexico.

Sam and the others who survived have always felt somewhat forgotten by the world and their country. To a large extent they were. Forty years after the war was over, the United States Army finally gave Sam Antonio and the other soldiers of Bataan and Corregidor the Bronze Star medal, with a "V" for valor. He and the others had earned it many times over.

In thinking about the horrors of war and his imprisonment, Sam also remembered those who were kind when their actions could have cost them their lives. There is the story of when he was struck by a Japanese guard who thought Sam was making fun of him. Without thinking, Sam struck back, but fortunately did not make contact. That would have meant an instant death sentence. The guard reported what had happened to an officer. Sam's punishment was severe. Sam was made to stand at strict attention for twenty-four hours with a bayonet, attached to a rifle, placed upright, just under his chin. If he nodded off to sleep, his head would fall and he would impale himself through his head. Sam stayed awake most of the time. He did start to nod off, and that's how he stabbed himself through the chin just under his tongue. He still has the scar. But even in war's profanity, Sam found decency.

The guards who watched over him stood two-hour shifts. Two separate guards during that time allowed Sam to lie down and sleep for almost their entire shifts. Sam said that if they had not done this, he surely would not have survived that ordeal. Had the guards been caught, they would probably have been killed.

Today Sam enjoys his family in Grants, New Mexico. He still has an occasional nightmare and there are times he still can't talk about some of the things that he witnessed. But he has kept his sense of humor. While driving through Grants, he spoke of the "Cow Pasture Poole Table" (the golf course) the city has placed on perfectly good desert land. But most of all Sam has retained his Acoma dignity. He still values those traditions taught to him by his mother and father, which he has passed along to his daughters and son. He hopes that his great-grandson "Little Sammy" will one day learn about his people. There is a good chance of that, because Sam's granddaughter Tina and "Little Sammy" live with him.

Sam recently bought a four-wheel all terrain vehicle for hunting. In the summer of 1997 Sam Antonio was a recipient of another medal. He won a gold medal in the Senior Citizens Olympics in archery. He also set a new state record using a fifty-pound compound bow. He attributes his great aim to all those carrots he ate while at Mukden Prison in Manchuria.

Shoichi Yokoi

The Last Japanese Soldier

In contrast to Sam Antonio, who was the last of his Acoma people to survive Bataan and Corregidor, Shoichi Yokoi became a national hero to Japan, twenty-seven years after the war had ended. He was discovered in a remote area of Guam on January 24, 1972. He did not know that World War II was over and that Japan had surrendered!

Long presumed dead, "Sergeant" Shoichi Yokoi was captured by two local hunters who had followed him to a fish trap in a river. The story that came out of the jungle was incredible.

Shoichi Yokoi was a Japanese soldier who refused to surrender after a fierce battle with U.S. troops in 1944. He hid in the remote jungles of Guam, where he lived alone in a cave on a diet of rats, frogs, snails, fish, wild nuts, and fruit. He had been a tailor's apprentice before being conscripted, and he made himself trousers and shirts with material he wove from bark fibers. He was in remarkably good health when he was found.

Although he had found newspapers saying that Japan had surrendered, Shoichi Yokoi had dismissed them as American propaganda. Within a month of his capture, he was sent back to Tokyo, Japan, where he received a hero's welcome. To Americans who witnessed the event, it was an incredible sight.

Ernie Novey, an Air Force Master Sergeant stationed at Fuchu Air Force Base in Tokyo, watched the elation of the Japanese he worked with on the radar units. Here in the midst of Japan's renaissance, an emerging technological giant in the modern world, arose the last vestige of the ancient samurai spirit. This lone, defiant soldier embodied all that was Japan. Not since Yukio Mishima committed *seppuku* (commonly referred to as *hari kari*) on a balcony in downtown Tokyo in early December 1970 had someone captured the attention of those who had lived in Japan's past.

Yukio Mishima, a best-selling author, playwright, and poet who had served in the war, publicly spoke out against Japan's entry into the twentieth century and its connection with the Western world. He considered himself the last samurai. On December 7, 1970, Yukio Mishima walked out onto a balcony in downtown Tokyo with a friend who acted as his second. (In the real world of the samurai, *seppuku* takes two.) Yukio Mishima pulled out his samurai short sword, stabbed himself in the abdomen, and made three very long cuts, disemboweling himself. His second then took the katana, the long samurai sword, raised it above his head with both hands, and swiftly cut off Mishima's head.

Shoichi Yokoi's message, on the other hand, was one of survival. He had not surrendered! He had been captured. A massive parade was planned and U.S. military personnel and civilian workers were not ordered, but strongly recommended, by the commander of the 8th United States Air Force, to keep a low profile on what had become an unofficial national holiday in all of Japan. The visibility of U.S. forces was a constant reminder to many Japanese that Americans were the victors in World War II.

No one in the recent history of Japan could remember a parade of this magnitude. It carried the very confused Shoichi Yokoi down through Tokyo's streets past millions of adoring countrymen. The parade ended in front of the Imperial Palace of Emperor Hirohito. It was there that the sergeant was greeted by the emperor, considered a deity by the Japanese during World War II. Shoichi Yokoi was now in the presence of his former god-emperor.

Shoichi Yokoi presented his rifle to the emperor and expressed his shame at returning home alive. He, like hundreds of thousands of

Japanese soldiers, had vowed never to be captured alive by enemy forces. Emperor Hirohito took the rifle and told Shoichi Yokoi that there was no shame and that his mere survival spoke for itself as to what kind of soldier he had been. Shoichi Yokoi was the living spirit that had rekindled a national pride, which had burned down to a mere ember. Japan no longer followed the code of the Bushido, for it no longer even had armed forces.

After Shoichi Yokoi was reunited with his surviving family, he was brought up to date about what had happened during his twenty-seven year absence. He was horrified that two Japanese cities had been destroyed by atomic bombs, but he marveled that man had walked on the moon only three years before his return to Japan. Shoichi Yokoi was amazed that his country was now one of the world's leaders in technology. Women had been given the right to vote, and rock and roll and country music had invaded his country.

During the next twenty-five years, Shoichi Yokoi lived a quiet life in retirement. On September 25, 1997, he died in a Japanese hospital of heart failure. Shoichi Yokoi, the last soldier of the Imperial Japanese Army, was eighty-two.

The Last Officer to Surrender

Two years after Shoichi Yokoi was captured in Guam, Lieutenant Hiroo Onoda was finally coaxed out of hiding in the Philippine jungles. When he was asked why he had not come out thirty years before, he stated that, unlike Shoichi Yokoi, he had never been informed that the war was over. And besides, he said, "I had not received the order to surrender."

Upon returning to Japan, Hiroo Onoda was also treated to a hero's welcome.

14

One Extraordinary Event

The Day They Hanged an Elephant

Author's note: About twelve years ago, I met and worked with an incredible storyteller named Jackie Torrence. We were in San Diego, California. During a brief conversation with her, she asked me if I was going to be in Jonesboro, Tennessee, later that year for the National Storytelling Festival. I said "yes" and she suggested that we get together there for either lunch or dinner. Then she asked me where I was going to be staying. Not being familiar with that part of eastern Tennessee, I informed her that I was going to be in a little town called "Erwin" and that I would be staying in a place called "The Family Inns." Her momentary silence was followed with "Oh."

"What do you mean 'Oh', Jackie?" I asked.

"Pat, that's a mean town."

Being with a master storyteller and expecting a joke, I asked, "How mean is the town?"

With a deadpan expression she said, "Pat, that town is so mean that they don't allow any black people in there and they hung an elephant!"

Not quite believing what I had just heard, I asked Jackie, "How do you hang an elephant and why would you?"

Jackie then said, "I don't rightly know. Besides that I'm black and they won't allow me in town to find out."

Totally flabbergasted, I looked at her and said, "Well Jackie, I reckon I'll have to find out for you."

A month later, after I arrived in Erwin, I finally asked the front desk clerk at The Family Inns, "Did you guys hang an elephant here? And if so, how and why did you do it?"

The desk clerk looked at me and reluctantly said, "Yes sir, we did, but it happened a long time ago. I don't know all the details of it, but my mother works down at the library and she's got a thick stack of papers in a file. She knows all about it. Would you like to go down and talk to her?"

I said that I would and went downtown to the public library. What follows is a true but unbelievable tale of how Mary, an African elephant, was hanged.

It all began in September 1916. The Sparks Circus had just come to Kingsport, Tennessee, for a few days. Crowds of folks from all over eastern Tennessee and western North Carolina and Virginia filled the big top circus tent. There were lions and tigers and bears (oh my!), clowns and elephants. And among those elephants was a 10,000-pound African elephant named Mary.

Now in those days, most animal trainers believed that the only way to train a wild animal was to beat it into submission. And on this particularly hot September Saturday, Mary had an inexperienced trainer working with her. While he was bringing her from one ring of the circus to another, Mary spotted a large pile of watermelon rinds that people had discarded. Now this elephant loved watermelon and its rind. As she started over to the pile of rinds, the new trainer, instead of trying to guide her away from the rinds with his trainer's stick, started beating her with it. All this did was make Mary the elephant mad. In an instant, she turned on the trainer, grabbed him with her trunk, and threw him to the ground. Then she stomped on him, making him a mushy spot on the ground. Some of the people who witnessed this had guns with them and they started shooting Mary. Their bullets did not penetrate her thick hide. Fortunately for everyone there, Mary did not go berserk. She stood there gorging herself on a feast of watermelon rinds. A more experienced trainer finally arrived and patiently waited for her to get her fill. Then and only then did he attempt to guide her to another area, where her feet were chained to the ground.

The public was outraged, and a judge in Kingsport said, "By God, that's murder! We're gonna have a trial!" And with that statement Mary the elephant was promptly charged with first degree murder. A trial was slated for Monday morning and Mary was found guilty and sentenced to die! At first the judge ruled that Mary would be shot to death, but nobody in that part of Tennessee had a gun big enough to shoot the elephant. The next idea for Mary's death proved to be far too cruel even for the judge. Someone suggested that the elephant be laid down between two railroad engines, facing opposite directions, with chains tied around her neck and body. Then they would have the engines start up and pull her head from her body. That idea was just too cruel, even for the judge who sentenced her to die. Then somebody spoke up and said, "Why don't we hang her?"

That was a great idea, someone else said, but then asked, "How do you hang a 10,000-pound elephant?"

"It's easy!" said the first man. "Down in Erwin, forty miles away, there's the Clinchfield Railroad yard, and in that yard there's a railroad crane. If that crane can pick up a railroad car, surely it can pick up an elephant! Let's bring that crane up here and hang the elephant!"

"That's the dumbest thing I've ever heard!" said yet another man. "It's easier to take the elephant down to the crane than it is to bring that crane up here."

Everyone agreed, and on September 13, 1916, a huge crowd gathered around Mary the elephant as her executioners wrapped a huge chain around her neck. The chain was attached to the railroad crane, which then hoisted the 10,000-pound pachyderm off her feet. She slowly strangled to death, thus making Erwin, Tennessee the only town in the recorded history of the world to hang an elephant.

The Hartleypoole Chimp Incident

During the Boer War, off the coast of Hartleypoole, England, a German ship was wrecked in a storm. All hands perished in the cold and terrible waters of the North Sea. The only survivor was a pet chimpanzee. Having never seen a chimpanzee before, the people of Hartleypoole immediately set out to capture this wild looking "man-beast." After they captured the poor, frightened animal, they tried it for espionage, because it had come from a German ship. The chimp was found guilty and was promptly hanged as a "German spy."

To this day, a hundred years later, Hartleypoole still takes a lot of ridicule from the rest of England, particularly before and after soccer games. The people of the town are still called "monkey hangers" or "monkey killers."

15

Governor Ralph Carr

A Man of Compassion

Some heroes are forgotten men, except by those they've saved. For thousands of Japanese Americans, Colorado Governor Ralph Carr will never be forgotten. He was a wartime hero who was never in the war, but he happened to be in the right place at the right time. He ignored personal risk and did something because it needed to be done and because it was truly right.

On Sunday, December 7, 1941, the Imperial Japanese Navy launched a surprise attack on military and civilian personnel at Pearl Harbor, Hawaii. Over 2,000 people were killed and the United States was plunged into World War II. Widespread panic swept over the United States, especially on the West Coast. On December 8, 1941, President Franklin Delano Roosevelt, before a Joint Session of Congress, asked for a declaration of war against Japan, Germany, and Italy. The vote was almost unanimous (the lone descending vote belonged to Montana Congresswoman Jeannette Pickering Rankin).

Roosevelt then put into action one of this country's most controversial laws: the Relocation Act. All Japanese in the United States were to be forced from their homes and placed in relocation camps. This edict included all Japanese, including those who were American citizens! Many of these people were not naturalized citizens, but were in fact born and raised in this country, and had fathers, grandfathers, or in many cases great-grandfathers who had immigrated here or were born here.

The media and racism helped the panic spread in the first couple of days following Pearl Harbor. The California state government ordered the Japanese to leave. Those who did not would be imprisoned. The first roundup of Japanese Americans began in and around the Los Angeles, California, area. Five hundred Japanese Americans were placed under guard at the Santa Anita racetrack.

Frank Torizawa, now owner of the Grenada Fish Market in Sakura Square in Denver, Colorado, was one of those people. He was living in California at that time, and after five months at Santa Anita, he was shipped off to Camp Amache, near Lamar, Colorado. He couldn't believe what had happened to him. Camp Amache was surrounded by barbed wire and there was a tower with soldiers carrying rifles and mounted machine guns. It was what it appeared to be, a prison camp.

Those Japanese Americans who did not voluntarily leave California were later rounded up by soldiers, the FBI, and police, who took them from their homes, put them in railroad cars, and shipped them to relocation camps. Mistakes were made. In one case a Navajo Indian who was working in California was mistaken for a Japanese American and sent to an internment camp for four weeks, until he could prove who he was.

Those Japanese Americans who did leave California were not welcomed anywhere they traveled. Many were forced to sleep in cars or camp along the highways. Food service was refused them in restaurants all over the west.

The *Rocky Mountain News* in Denver made the situation worse by running a wire-service article by a man identified as "one of America's best known anthropologists," who explained that Japanese "have a clever, smarter expression, the reflection of their materialistic and commercial interests," while Chinese faces are "mild and friendly and interesting." The *News* also ran a picture of a man in Julesburg, Colorado, identified as a "cowboy," holding a large Bowie knife, while proclaiming, "Japs is just like injuns." In another article, a Weld County woman identified as "Rattlesnake Kate" said that she was prepared to take on the Japanese with shotgun, rifle, or club.

It was amid this hysteria and hatred that calm and compassion quickly surfaced. Its source was the honorable Ralph L. Carr, governor of the state of Colorado. He was the one western governor who reminded people that the refugees, who were streaming eastward from California, had the same rights as others guaranteed by the U.S. Constitution.

On December 10, 1941, just three days after the Japanese bombed Pearl Harbor, Governor Carr told the people of Colorado in a radio broadcast that, "We cannot test the degree of a man's affection for his fellows or his country by the birthplace of his grandfather." The governor also told the public that Colorado would welcome the Japanese Americans and that no Coloradan of Japanese ancestry would be deprived of his basic freedoms. He took the words in the U.S. Constitution seriously: "that all men are created equal and have equal rights before the law. ... They are loyal Americans, sharing only race with the enemy."

The press, the public, and the state legislature went wild. Hate letters and threats were addressed to the governor from people bitterly opposed to his welcoming the "Japs" to Colorado. Denver City Councilman H.C. Dolph said, "I am opposed to any Japanese being brought into the state for any reason." Colorado Senator Ed Johnson stated that the Colorado National Guard should be called out to keep Japanese Americans out of Colorado. One Denver woman wrote a letter to the *Denver Post* stating that, "Colorado was becoming a dumping ground for sneaking Japs" and "if California wants to get rid of them, why not dump them into the ocean?" But Carr would not change his stance, which was based on courage and knowledge.

Ralph L. Carr was born in the San Luis Valley of Colorado in a little town called Rosita, on December 11, 1887. During his lifetime he had carried samples of mine assays and had been a grocery clerk, a telegraph operator, a laundry wagon driver, a newspaper reporter and then an editor. He then attended law school and was admitted to the bar in 1912.

Carr opened up a law office in Antonito, Colorado, in 1916 and quickly became involved with the town council and the school board, and later became the county attorney. He became well versed in water law, Spanish land law, and Hispanic culture. Having grown up in this mostly Hispanic valley, Ralph Carr knew the Spanish language. Whenever the Hispanic population had a problem, they went to him. Throughout his life he maintained life-long friendships in this community.

Just fourteen miles north of Antonito was another small town, La Jara. It was here that Carr had his first contact with Japanese Americans. He got to know the residents and their culture well. Their kindness and gentleness stayed with Carr for the rest of his life.

Ralph Carr's talents and intellect eventually took him away from the San Luis Valley. His expertise in water law led to his appointment as the assistant attorney general of Colorado and then later to an appointment by President Herbert Hoover as the U.S. Attorney for the District of Colorado. In 1938 he was drafted by the Republican Party to run for governor of Colorado. He agreed, reluctantly. His use of the radio and his eloquence as a speaker appealed to Colorado voters. Ralph Carr was the first Republican to be elected to that office in fourteen years.

During his first term, Carr accomplished an incredible amount for the people of Colorado. While the rest of the country was in the grip of the Great Depression, Carr was able to successfully transfer 65 percent of the state income taxes from the school fund to the general fund to erase a $2 million state deficit. He spoke out against federal encroachments on state rights and called out the National Guard to quell the violence that erupted during a labor dispute at a reservoir site in western Colorado. Ralph Carr had become an extremely effective and popular governor. Carr's reputation brought him to national attention, and in 1940 he easily won his bid for re-election.

Although known as the "businessman's governor," Carr always cared about everyday folks. As an ardent student of Abraham Lincoln,

Carr cherished individual rights and equal protection under the law. It was this love of law and the memory of the Japanese Americans he'd known in La Jara that made Carr cast aside all the pressure heaped upon him during those first unforgettable days of World War II.

During 1942, the first full year of U.S. participation in World War II, as Carr fought off the public's hysteria, U.S. forces in the South Pacific were being defeated in every enemy engagement. Bataan and Corregidor and the rest of the Philippine islands had fallen after President Roosevelt ordered General Douglas MacArthur to escape to Australia. Plus most of the United States Navy's Pacific Fleet lay below the waters of Pearl Harbor. "What," the public asked, "would prevent an invasion of the West Coast?" Despite all this looming over the nation, Carr stood fast on his invitation to the Japanese Americans fleeing California to settle in Colorado. As many as 30,000 evacuees eventually settled in Colorado.

Carr further outraged Colorado citizens when he hired a Japanese American from Camp Amache as his housekeeper. He chose a young woman who had been forced to interrupt her studies at the University of California. While working for the governor she was able to complete her studies at the University of Denver. When she graduated, the governor hired another Amache internee. One neighbor of the Governor's Mansion wondered how the governor and his family could sleep under the same roof with a "Jap."

In mid-1942, after the news of U. S. victories at Midway and Coral Sea, public hysteria died down. Merchants in Lamar, Colorado, began erecting signs welcoming trade with the 8,000 Japanese Americans from Camp Amache, who were now given frequent leaves into town. The townspeople quickly found out that these "prisoners" were very quiet and gracious. They were also the biggest spenders.

Many citizens of Colorado had calmed down, but the majority, who had no contact with Japanese Americans, held onto their anger when they went to the voting polls when Ralph Carr ran for re-election. Carr had committed political suicide. But he had known that when he made his speech on December 10, 1941, three days after Pearl Harbor and the day before his birthday.

After the war ended, Carr continued with his law practice, where he represented both the wealthy and the poor with great fervor until he suddenly died of a heart attack on September 23, 1950.

Carr never forgot his roots or the significance of the Constitution. And the Japanese Americans never forgot Ralph Carr. In 1979, Japanese Americans in Colorado got together and created the Japanese Cultural Center, called Sakura Square, at 19th and Larimer Streets in Denver. In their courtyard they unveiled a $25,000 bronze bust of Governor Ralph L. Carr. This was not their only commemoration of this man.

December 11, 1987, marked the 100th birthday of Governor Carr. On that cold, wintry day some twenty Japanese Americans stood and bowed in front of that bronze bust. They had come to mark the birth of a man who offered them a place to come when all others had rejected them. The Reverend Joseph Sakakibara recalled an old Japanese belief that you "should never forget a gratitude or a favor," and then added, "As long as we're alive, we should never forget those who helped us when we were in need." Ralph Carr has been forgotten by many of Colorado's history teachers, but not by the Japanese Americans in Colorado.

Interesting Facts about the Internment Camps

1.   Many of the young men who were interned volunteered to join the United States Army. In 1943, they were put in an all-Japanese-American unit call the 442nd Regimental Combat Unit. They trained at Camp Shelby, Mississippi, and fought in the European theater, becoming the most decorated fighting unit in U.S. history. Over 9,000 of these men gave their lives for their country, while many of their relatives were interned and had their homes and property taken from them.

2.   In September 1987, Congress formally apologized to Japanese Americans and authorized a payment of $20,000 to each of the camp's survivors.

3.   When this author was interviewing survivors of Camp Amache and their children at Sakura Square, he first asked the question "What is your definition of a 'hero'?" With almost no exceptions, they pointed at the door leading to Ralph Carr's bust or spoke his name.

16

Jeannette Pickering Rankin

The Lady from Montana

A s a child in Montana, Jeannette Rankin loved to hear the stories that her father John told, especially the one about Chief Joseph of the Nez Perce. Her father told her that the famous chief was confronted by an army captain and his troops, who demanded his surrender. Her father said that the great chief asked for time to think about it, and the captain agreed. Evening came, but when the next morning arrived, both the darkness and the Nez Perce had vanished over the mountains. A battle had been averted and no lives were taken. Her father told Jeannette this tale many times, and knew it to be true, for he had been a member of those troops. From this story a value for human life was instilled in young Jeannette. And from that time on she wanted to do something with her life that would be meaningful to others.

Jeannette Rankin had no idea at the time that this story had planted the seeds of world peace in her mind. She would use her intellect and charm to rise above those political obstacles placed in her path. In 1916, Jeannette Pickering Rankin became the first woman in U.S. history to be elected to the U.S. House of Representatives. And she accomplished this feat four years before women were given the right to vote!

Born on a Missoula, Montana, ranch on June 11, 1880, Jeannette was the oldest of the seven children born to John and Olive Rankin. Throughout her childhood she heard tales about her western culture from her father. She was in fact a "daddy's girl." Even though her family was well off, Jeannette and her siblings were not spoiled. They all had chores to do; Jeannette's included chopping wood, clearing brush, and starting fires. She also worked with horses. Jeannette could ride a horse as well as any man and got to know the ways of cattle barons and cowboys. She was also called upon to do some "horse stitching." Once, when still a teenager, Jeannette was asked by her father to sew up a horse named Star. The horse's flesh had been severely torn by a barbed wire fence. With the talents of a superb seamstress, Jeannette stitched the horse back together.

Jeannette Rankin was first introduced to poverty when she visited some of the nearby Indian reservations. Here she saw the once proud people of the plains living in shacks and off the corrupt welfare system that had been created by the Bureau of Indian Affairs and the U.S. government.

This was a sight Rankin would never forget. She knew that she wanted to do something more with her life than to be a school teacher or a rancher's wife, the only two options open to a young woman in the late nineteenth century in the West. After she graduated from high school, Jeannette attended and graduated from the University of Montana with a B.S. in biology. She was twenty-two.

After teaching school for one year, Jeannette Rankin moved to Missoula, Montana. There she worked as a dressmaker, but Fate intervened in that year of 1904. Her younger brother Wellington was attending Harvard University and invited Jeannette to come out for a visit. She couldn't wait. Rankin had never been out of Montana. This was her chance to visit the big city and see, hear, and feel all of the things her brother had written about in his many letters.

Once she arrived in Boston, Rankin was greeted by her favorite sibling and a sight that would forever change her life. During her carriage ride from the train station to her brother's apartment, she witnessed mass poverty for the first time. And that poverty overwhelmed her every sense. It wasn't anything like the Indian reservations. In her Montana isolation she had equated the poor with the native people who once freely roamed the land. Here in Boston, though, the poverty that met her spread through the tenement houses like a cancer upon the very city where the American Revolution had begun (the Boston Massacre). After getting over the initial shock of the poor's misery, Rankin was introduced to the literary life Harvard University offered her brother. Through Wellington she was given access to the university's huge library. The majority of her visit was spent there in the quiet, but what she read tore at emotions. She began reading protest literature and about reformers such as Jane Addams of Hull House in Chicago. Something urged her to be of use, not as a teacher, but as an active participant to clean up the slums of cities and to offer some sort of education to the poor.

Jeannette Rankin soon left Boston and went to New York City to attend the New York School of Philanthropy. After graduating, she was offered a job at an orphan home in Spokane, Washington. Rankin was appalled at the harsh treatment of the children, but couldn't change anything in the male-dominated society of that period. It was here that she began her career in politics, determined to change things for women and children.

From Spokane, Rankin moved to Seattle, where she attended the University of Washington. While there, she volunteered to work at the Washington Equal Suffrage Association. She began by putting posters for women's suffrage in places like barber shops and other male-oriented businesses. Much to the surprise of everyone in the association, Rankin had sweet talked the owners of those places into helping her.

This was only her first step in the suffrage movement. Rankin was instrumental in getting Washington State to pass a women's suffrage amendment to their state constitution. Energized by this victory, she went home to Montana in 1911 and became the first woman in the State's history to be allowed to address the state legislature on the subject of equal rights for women.

Rankin's speech was rousing and yet touching to her home state's lawmakers and she received a standing ovation. However, she was not able to convince enough of the legislative body to support a suffrage amendment to Montana's constitution. The vote was close. This did not discourage Rankin. Her efforts in Montana took her away from her home again.

Jeannette Rankin's talents in the political arena caught the attention of national suffrage leaders, and from Montana she began traveling the country giving speeches on behalf of the National American Woman Suffrage Association. Rankin continued with this agenda and three years after her speech in Montana helped to bring the suffrage movement to her home state.

In 1914, when World War I broke out in Europe, Jeannette Rankin helped found the Woman's Peace Party. She began dividing her time between the peace movement and the suffrage movement, and in 1915, traveled to New Zealand to study the effects of women's voting power in that country. What she learned greatly helped her in the following year when she decided to run as a Republican candidate for the U.S. House of Representatives.

No one thought she had a chance of winning, for no woman had ever been elected to national office. This did not stop Rankin. She knew the people of Montana and she now had the voting power of women in that state behind her. In November 1916, Jeannette Pickering Rankin won the election. She not only made state history, but became the very first woman in the history of the United States to be elected to the House of Representatives. That in itself was extraordinary, because most women in the United States still did not have the power of the vote!

During her two years in office, Rankin was instrumental in getting the 19th Amendment passed by both houses of Congress (in 1919). Although she was no longer in office, the House of Representatives passed the bill on May 21 and the Senate followed on June 4 of that year. The amendment simply read:

Article XIX,

Section 1

The right of citizens of the United States to vote shall not be denied or abridged by the United States or by any state on account of sex.

Section 2

Congress shall have the power to enforce this article by appropriate legislation.

This bill was originally submitted to Congress on January 10, 1878. It took forty years of hard work by women like Jeannette Rankin to get it into law. The 19th Amendment became law in 1920, the year after Jeannette Rankin was voted out of office.

Jeannette Rankin was one of the very few in Congress to vote against the United States entering World War I. She had never forgotten the story of Chief Joseph her father had told her. In her own mind she was convinced that there were alternative ways of settling political, religious, and racial conflicts without the use of violence. Her pacifist stand cost her her re-election bid.

Though politically defeated, Rankin's spirit continued to soar as she threw herself into other areas where champions were needed. For years she continued to speak out against war and poverty and became a lobbyist for the National Consumers League in 1923.

That same year, Jeannette Rankin moved to an area just outside of Athens, Georgia, and began building a small farm house. She had accepted a job there with the Women's International League for Peace and Freedom (WILPF). This was an organization Rankin cofounded in Zurich, Switzerland, while on a congressional trip there in 1919. Soon she began another organization called the Georgia Peace Society. While in yet another organization, the Works for Women's Peace Union, she lobbied Congress for a constitutional amendment to outlaw war.

Rankin continued her work for nearly ten years as a lobbyist and field secretary for the National Council for the Prevention of War. In 1939 she decided to go back to Montana and run for Congress once again. At age sixty she began a campaign as a pacifist in an America that did not want to be involved in the new war looming in Europe.

By the time Rankin was elected to her second term, Hitler had already started World War II. She was determined to keep America out of this war, but after the Japanese bombed Pearl Harbor on December 7, 1941, American sentiment turned against the pacifist stand. When Franklin D. Roosevelt asked the Congress of the United States for a declaration of war, the lone dissenting voice came from the "Lady from Montana": Jeannette Pickering Rankin. Again, in her bid for re-election she was defeated because of her anti-war stance.

In 1943 Rankin returned to Montana to take care of her elderly and ailing mother. While there, she also studied the nonviolence movement of Mahatma Gandhi. Shortly after her mother's death, Rankin began touring the world in search of the answer to world peace, but while in the United States she made Georgia her home.

During the next three years Jeannette Rankin made over six trips to India alone, hoping to meet Gandhi himself, but an assassin's bullet prevented their meeting. For the next seventeen years, Jeannette Rankin traveled to Western and Eastern Europe, Asia, South America, Africa, and Mexico promoting peace and equality for all peoples of all races and genders. When the war in Vietnam escalated in the 1960s, Jeannette became a very vocal opponent.

President John F. Kennedy's escalation of the war rankled the "Lady from Montana." The irony of this was that in 1958, the then-senator from Massachusetts had published an article titled "Three Women of Courage." In his article, Kennedy praised Jeannette Rankin: "Few members of Congress have ever stood more alone for being true to a higher honor and loyalty." As president, Kennedy never dreamed that this woman whom he had praised would speak out against his policies. Jeannette Rankin was now in her eighties.

For the next few years, Rankin continued her anti-war speeches and rallies. About a week before the bloodiest period in the Vietnam War, the 1968 Tet Offensive, she led her Jeannette Rankin Brigade into the heart of the nation's capital to protest the war. She continued to lobby Congress and speak out against the war, at one point threatening to run for Congress again.

In 1970, Rankin slipped on the stairs of a drugstore in Watkins-ville, Georgia. She had broken her hip. In typical "Rankin fashion," she was determined that this accident was not going to deter her from attending her own 90th birthday party in June in Congress. Although she wasn't able to walk, she was wheeled into the Rayburn House Office Building on June 11, 1970. Over 200 people had gathered there to pay tribute to the "Lady from Montana." She was praised by political allies and enemies alike for her integrity and courage. When it was time for her to speak, Rankin slowly rose up from her wheelchair and delivered an incredible speech. She used no notes. Her mind was still sharp and her voice articulate, even eloquent, when she thanked those gathered and then spoke of the future, not the past. Rankin herself would not linger in the past.

In 1972, at age 92, Jeannette Rankin delivered a rousing speech in a ceremony in which the National Organization for Women (NOW) inducted her as the first member of the Susan B. Anthony Hall of Fame. In that same year she publicly supported Councilwoman Shirley Chisholm's (the first African American woman elected to the U.S. Congress) bid for president of the United States.

In her lifetime Jeannette Rankin spoke out for equality for all people and the right of all American citizens to vote. She was deeply involved in the Civil Rights Movement and she spoke out against the four major wars she witnessed, in which the United States had been involved. Jeannette Pickering Rankin died in Carmel, California on May 18, 1973, just shy of her 93rd birthday. Although the cause of death was considered "heart failure," those who knew her would argue that her heart never failed, for it still lives in those who fight for peace and equality.

Her passing was peaceful and her ashes were scattered over the Pacific Ocean. This was appropriate, for the word "Pacific" means peaceful. A few months before her death, consumer advocate Ralph Nader said of her, "If aging is the erosion of one's ideals, then Jeannette Rankin is forever young."

Quotes from Jeannette Pickering Rankin

When a *New York Times* reporter asked Jeannette if she had to do it all over again, would she? "Yes," she said. "Only this time I'd be much nastier."

When asked about whether she considered Montana or Georgia as home, she answered, "I live on an airplane." This statement was in reference to how much she traveled.

"I have worked for suffrage for years, and got it. I've worked for peace for over fifty-five years and haven't come close."

"What one decides to do in crisis depends upon one's philosophy in life, and that philosophy, in crisis cannot be changed by an accident. If one hasn't any philosophy, in crisis others make the decision."

When voting against the United States' entry into World War II, Jeannette Rankin followed her "Nay" vote with the following statement: "As a woman, I cannot go to war, and I refuse to send anyone else!"

After her vote against war, Jeannette Rankin received thousands of letters filled with hate and name calling. She never allowed herself to be tainted by name calling. She personally answered all of that mail and explained her beliefs.

17

Villains

Lavinia Fisher

A lmost every history book claims that Mary Surrate was the first woman ever to be hanged in the United States. It's obvious that most of those writers of history have long overlooked Lavinia Fisher. She was hanged in Charleston, South Carolina, over forty years before Mary Surrate danced to the hangman's song.

No one knows where Lavinia Fisher or her husband John came from, but history does record what they did and how they died. In the years between 1810 and 1820, John and Lavinia Fisher were the owners of a "wayfarer house," or what would now be called a motel. It was called the Six Mile Wayfarer House, because it was exactly six miles from Charleston, South Carolina. It stood where the Old Dorchester Road crossed Goose Creek Road at Ashley Ferry.

By all accounts, Lavinia and John Fisher ran this house for a few years, and as the years passed, stories began to flourish about strange activities that occurred there. People who stayed there seemed to have disappeared, but when the sheriff checked out those reports, nothing out-of-line could be found. And John and Lavinia Fisher were always very friendly and helpful. They seemed to be a nice couple, and any- one who had ever seen Lavinia Fisher said that she was an incredibly beautiful woman. However, they could not understand what she was doing with a ruffian like John Fisher. Charleston folks who saw them said it really had to be a case of love gone mad. The Charlestonians all wondered why a woman who looked like Lavinia would associate with such rough looking men as her husband and his companions. Those questions always arose when they were in town, but they didn't come to town that often.

The Fishers prospered in those short years, more than anyone would have ever expected. Folks who traveled mentioned that they had stayed at the "Four Mile House" or one of the others, but it seemed that no one ever talked about staying at the "Six Mile" house. That was, until one night, when a man rode into Charleston as though the Devil himself was after him. It seems that the man, whose name was John Peeples, had survived an encounter with the owners of the Six Mile Wayfarer.

The day had been rainy, and as the night's blackness arose, the rain became a storm. John Peeples was weary from his journey and soon found himself confronting a lighted house. It was the Six Mile Wayfarer House. Although he had heard strange stories about this place, he was too tired to travel on to Charleston. He was met at the door by Lavinia Fisher, who asked him to come in. Peeples became nervous as soon as he entered the building. Sitting at a table were John Fisher and a couple of his friends. They were quite friendly with Peeples—too friendly. They offered to unsaddle his horse and bring in his belongings. They insisted.

After giving Peeples some dinner and ale, Lavinia Fisher volunteered to show him to his room for the night. She flirted with him all the way to the top of the stairs and then slowly opened the door to the room and showed him the bed. Laughing, she jumped and landed on his bed and said, "You should sleep well on this bed. If you need anything don't hesitate to ask." With that she winked at Peeples and slowly let herself out the door.

By now Peeples knew that something wasn't right. He looked at the bed. It was placed against a room wall and the outside wall, but was directly in front of the door he had entered with Lavinia Fisher. "It would be easy for them," he thought, "to slip into this room tonight and shoot me or stab me." He felt that if he didn't do something soon, he would never see the morning. Quickly, John Peeples took his bedroll from his belongings and with the pillow from the bed constructed a dummy in the bed. Then he sat up in a chair on the other side of the room, out of sight of the doorway. If John Fisher and his cronies came into the room, Peeples would at least have a fighting chance. His quick thinking saved his life.

No one came through the doorway that night. What happened, though, surprised Peeples so much that he jumped through the second floor window down to the ground. There he ran to the stables, jumped on his unsaddled horse, and rode as hard as it would take him to Charleston.

In the guest room, John Fisher had rigged up a false wall with a lever on the other side. With one mighty pull on the lever, the bed was turned completely over into a thirty-foot pit below the false floor. Anything or any person lying on that bed would be thrown down into that pit. Those people who weren't killed from the fall would later die from their injuries or from lack of food and water.

Once Peeples got to Charleston, he went to the sheriff's office and told him what had happened. By morning, the sheriff had arrived at the Six Mile Wayfarer's House and arrested John and Lavinia Fisher on a warrant sworn out by Peeples. When they searched the house they found the false floor and the remains of a "few" people. Some of the victims had been dumped there by the bed, while others had been poisoned by Lavinia or stabbed by John or his servant. More decomposing bodies and skeletal remains were found in the surrounding woods.

John and Lavinia Fisher and three others were tried and convicted of murder. Their sentence was to be "hanged by the neck until you are dead." In early January 1820, John Fisher was the first to be hanged. Lavinia Fisher thought that her beauty or gender might save her, as no woman had ever been hanged before in the young United States.

She found that neither would save her. She was taken to the gallows on the Meeting Street Road, where the Cooper River Bridge traffic now enters it. Asked if she had any last words, Lavinia Fisher, standing in the morning sun, taunted the crowd before her: "If ye have a message to send to Hell, give it to me—I'll carry it!"

The floor below her then opened and Lavinia Fisher fell victim to the hangman's noose and into the pages of legend and history.

Footnotes in Crime

1. The second woman in U.S. history to be hanged was Frances "Frankie" Silver of the Toe River area of North Carolina (near present-day Morganton, North Carolina). To make a long story short, on December 22, 1831, while her husband Charles lay sleeping on the floor with their baby daughter in his arms, Frankie gently removed the child from his arms and then removed her husband's head with an axe. She then chopped up the rest of his body in little pieces and burned them in the fireplace. Frankie Silver was arrested, tried, and convicted of murdering her husband. On July 12, 1832, she was taken to a gallows in Morganton, North Carolina, and hanged to death. Frankie's infant child was raised by Charles's relatives and lived well past her ninetieth birthday.

2. Bruce Barnes Jr., better known to the world as "Machine Gun Kelly," never fired a firearm at any human being during his lifetime, nor did he take a human life. His myth was created by his wife Katherine, who was also his partner in crime. Kelly did spend the last years of his life in federal prisons for the kidnapping of an Oklahoma City oil tycoon. He died in 1954 at the age of 57, of a heart attack.

Those Weren't Ladies, They Were Pirates

Anne Bonny and Mary Read

N ot much is known about these two women's early lives. What is known about Anne Bonny is that she was born in County Cork, Ireland, the illegitimate daughter of a lawyer and a maid-servant. This birth caused a scandal, which forced Anne's father to take his new family to the Carolinas sometime in the early part of the 1700s. This period of time was probably the most calm in her tumultuous life. What is known after this is that Anne went to sea as a sailor when she was about sixteen.

Growing up in the coastal areas of South Carolina, Anne had always yearned to be at sea, but knew that as a young woman it would be almost impossible. One day though, she had an idea. If she could disguise herself as a young man it would be possible to sign onto a crew. It wasn't just any crew that she wanted to join. Anne wanted to be a pirate. Throughout her area pirates created fear amongst all sea-faring men except those in the British Navy.

Stories abounded about men like Captain Robert Morgan and the monster of a man called Blackbeard. He was the newest threat to the area and he seemed invincible. Almost 300 pounds of muscle and nearly seven feet tall, Blackbeard had created an incredible image and reputation for himself. It was said by those who'd seen him that his long black beard was braided with red ribbons tied around the end of them, while beneath his hat he would place lit, slow burning fuses from his canons. The effect this made, with smoke arising from underneath his hat and his huge muscled body, made Blackbeard look like the devil himself.

The adventures and possibilities of this lifestyle were irresistible to young Anne. So one day, disguised as a young man, she signed on to a crew that was leaving for the Caribbean. The ship's first stop was Port Royal, Jamaica. Anne soon found a pirate crew that accepted her and made friends with a young man about her age. The two found themselves strangely attracted to each other. Their friendship deepened and one night, as they undressed, they were shocked to find that they were both women! Her friend turned out to be Mary Read. She too had longed to be a pirate. The two sailed with each other for months and soon became acquainted with none other than Edward Teach, Blackbeard himself, and other pirates like Major Stede Bonnet, of whom it was said that he bought his own ship (not usually done, because pirates stole their ships) to escape a nagging wife.

Anne and Mary found out the true stories behind the fables at the same time that they began creating their own legends. It was said that both women were superb with either cutlass or pistol and could hold their own in the thick of battle. Eventually Anne married another pirate, James Bonny. But after he was pardoned Bonny led a sober life, and Anne got bored. She took up with another pirate, Jack Rackham, called "Calico Jack" because of his loud clothes. He fell madly in love with Anne and lavished gifts of gold and jewels on her. After his money ran out, Rackham ignored his pardon and returned to his pirating ways, this time with Anne.

Although Anne had left James Bonny, she kept his last name. She and "Calico Jack" Rackham teamed up and returned to sea as pirates.

Still dressed as a man, Anne proved herself an exceptional "seaman." Few people knew that she was a woman.

In November 1720, luck ran out for Anne, Calico Jack, and another pirate aboard Rackham's ship: Mary Read. Captured at sea by British Captain Jonathan Barrett, Rackham and his crew were taken to the town of St. Jago de la Vega in Jamaica. They were tried before a court of the Admiralty and found guilty of piracy under the Act of 11 and 12 William III. Rackham and twelve male members of his crew were then "hung on Gibbits in Chains, for publick Example, and to terrify others from such-like evil Practices." Rackham and his crew were executed in Port Royal, Jamaica, on November 18, 1720, and their bodies strung up at various points around the island.

Two days later, Anne Bonny and Mary Read were tried in the same Court of the Admiralty, with Sir Nicholas Lawes, governor of Jamaica, presiding. Neither Anne nor Mary chose to testify or interrogate witnesses in their defense. The commissioners of the court unanimously found them guilty of "piracies, robberies and felonies," as charged in the third and fourth items of the articles of piracy.

Governor Lawes then sentenced both women to be hanged until dead. As soon as he pronounced the sentence, both Anne and Mary immediately informed the court that they were "quick with child and prayed that the execution of the said sentence should be respited, and that an inspection should be made." Governor Lawes immediately ordered the two women examined by a physician. His pronounced that both Anne and Mary were indeed with child and that the executions should be delayed until after they gave birth.

Not long after the trial, Mary Read came down with a "violent" fever in prison and died without giving birth. Anne Bonny was given several reprieves and did give birth to a child. History did not record the gender of the child or what happened to Anne Bonny after she was released from prison. We do know that Anne Bonny and Mary Read were the only two female pirates in U.S. history.

Pirate Briefs

1. After Edward Teach came to the American continent in 1716, he was better known to the world as "Blackbeard the Pirate." He was almost seven feet tall and weighed close to 300 pounds. For two years he roamed North Carolina's Outer Banks. From there he sailed to the Caribbean coasts, from Port Royal to Key West back up to Charleston, South Carolina. He had a home in Bath, North Carolina and was protected by the colonial governor.

In May 1718, Blackbeard held the city of Charleston for ransom. He had captured twenty-one of Charleston's most prominent citizens at sea and threatened to kill them if the city did not meet his demands. The city allowed Blackbeard's crew to enter their domain to retrieve whatever they desired. When the pirates' foray had ended, Blackbeard released his hostages in only their underwear.

On about December 17, 1718, Blackbeard met his bloody end in a battle with the British Navy in Ocracoke Inlet, North Carolina. Lieutenant Robert Maynard's crew caught up with Blackbeard's ship in the shallows. After a brief fight at sea, Maynard's crew boarded Blackbeard's ship. The bloody, hand-to-hand fighting continued for about two hours. During this time Blackbeard, though wounded, viciously continued fighting. Finally the first mate of Lieutenant Maynard's crew took a cleaving axe to the side of the giant pirate's neck and severed his jugular vein. But Blackbeard continued to fight until Lieutenant Maynard's crew closed in on him. Finally, after losing a great deal of blood from his neck wound and thirty-two other wounds, Edward Teach died. Lieutenant Maynard then ordered Blackbeard's head severed from his body and had it placed on the bowsprit of the lieutenant's ship. The head was taken to Virginia to show Governor Spotswood that the pirate was in fact dead.

Blackbeard's skull dangled from a pole on the mouth of the Hampton River in Virginia for many years as a warning to those who might think of becoming pirates. Later the skull was taken down and used as a base for a large punch bowl.

2. Most pirates started their careers as privateers. These were private sailors and captains hired out by the British government to wreak havoc on French and Spanish merchant ships during the wars. When the wars ended, these privateers became self-employed as pirates.

Jonita

28 September 1950

Dear Mother and Daddy,

I suppose you have my telegram now. I'm really not too badly hurt. I have both arms broken, so I suppose you really don't have to worry about my flying anymore—at least for quite some time.

Remember when I was stationed at the 118th? That's where I'm in the hospital right now, although I expect to go to Tokyo soon.

There isn't a lot to write you about. Looks like we're winning the war. Maybe, I'll even get to come home before my tour is over.

A lady from the Red Cross is writing this for me, so don't expect too many letters. Do write real often though—same address.

Love,

Jonita

Jonita's letter was the kind of letter that people write when they don't want loved ones to worry. But before this letter arrived, Jonita Bonham's parents had already received the official telegram the United States Air Force had sent. Ironically, the telegram arrived only moments after the Bonhams had returned home from a movie theater in Oklahoma City, where they had seen their daughter, Lieutenant Jonita Ruth Bonham, an air evacuation nurse, in a newsreel. Jonita Bonham appeared on screen stepping off her plane—a C-54, in Korea. The telegram was a shock to the Bonhams. Their daughter was "seriously ill in a Japanese hospital since September 26, when she was injured in an aircraft accident." That's all the telegram said. It did not mention that twenty-six people, including the pilot and the other flight nurse, Vera Brown, had been killed in the "accident." Vera Brown had been sitting next to Jonita Bonham. Out of the fifty-four people on that plane, only twenty-eight survived.

The telegram also didn't tell mention the kinds of hours the flight teams were putting in and the conditions around them. In the two weeks previous to the crash, Jonita Bonham and her crew had been aloft for 245 hours and had evacuated over 600 wounded from Korea to hospitals in Japan. There had been no days off or sleep for her crew except for the token three-hour naps between flights. The telegram didn't mention the amount of enemy fire their plane took every time it landed or took off in "hot LZs" (landing zones).

The first taste of Jonita's reality reached the Bonhams when they received a letter from Doctor Clifford Boveé, Major, M.S.C., dated September 28, 1950:

> Dear Mr. & Mrs. Bonham—
> Your daughter is making a splendid recovery from the injuries she sustained in the airplane crash last Tuesday morning. She suffered a broken left forearm, a fracture of the right shoulder blade and some painful lacerations of the scalp, with, of course, a general shaking up and numerous bruises and scratches. However, there is nothing critical nor of a permanent nature about her condition.

The doctor's letter continued with information about what hospital she was in and when she would be transferred to in Tokyo. On the second page he described how the crash occurred and then mentioned what Jonita had done immediately after the plane broke apart on impact:

You may be very proud of your splendid daughter. She won the respect and admiration of everyone for her courage, bravery, resourcefulness and clear-thinking during the disastrous tragedy. Following the crash, and despite her own suffering, she reacted so quickly to the emergency that she succeeded in getting life rafts launched and directed their loading during the few moments before the plane sank. Had it not been for her courage and presence of mind, it was the unanimous opinion of all that there would not have been half the survivors there were from the crash.

I trust there is nothing contained in this letter which may give you any cause for alarm, for rest assured that you need have none. ... She will be hospitalized for probably two or three weeks to allow the fractures to knit.

Within ten days the Bonhams received another letter, this time from Jonita, who never mentioned what she had done during the crash.

Saturday 7 Sept 50

[Author's note: It was actually Oct. 7, 1950. The crash occurred on Sept. 26, 1950. The enveloped was postmarked Oct. 9, 1950.]

Dear Mother and Daddy,

I haven't heard from you all since the plane crash, but I know shall just most any time—and since I feel pretty good today I'm going to try and write you all about it.

I hope you can read this scribbling, but I'm flat in bed and my right arm is broken at the shoulder, so I can't move it except for the fingers. My left wrist is broken too—so when they put my right shoulder in a splint I'm not going to able to do anything.

One thing I didn't tell you—I got a skull fracture out of the accident, but I've already had the surgery done, and it's perfectly all right. I also got a big cut on my cheek which is going to call for a little plastic work. It's really not bad at all tho' as it is— I shall be coming back to the states tho' sooner. And I'm absolutely through with flying—which you will be probably glad to hear.

Our crash was on take off and we crashed into the water. We were taking troops into Kimpo. There were about 50 some on the plane & about 28 of us were saved. So—see, I really was very lucky. ... If they splint my arm soon I'll have the Red Cross write you soon.

Love Always,

Jonita

Again Jonita Bonham understated the extent of her injuries. Even though she said nothing about her actions in the early morning hours of September 126, 950, word of her heroics was spread by crash survivors, not only to the press, but to Air Force officials.

Pfc. Percy Johnson, a hardened combat veteran returning to the front lines of Korea, who survived the crash, wrote in his official report to the Air Force: "Lieutenant Bonham took command. None of us guessed that she was badly hurt. She wasn't excited and she used her head. All the men took orders from her without question. She saved a lot of guys."

The facts of this incident spread faster than rumors on a ship at sea. And the facts were more incredible than fiction. In the early morning hours of September 26, 1950, Lieutenant Jonita Bonham woke up from her three-hour nap. She heated up and drank two strong cups of black coffee, the kind that would take rust off a forty-year-old wreck. After this brief respite, Bonham headed for flight operations. As she stepped outside she noticed the wind. It began howling through the compound. The wind felt and blew as though a storm were brewing, but there was no rain. When Jonita Bonham reported to flight operations in the darkness of pre-dawn, she could hear the throbbing engines of a half dozen cargo planes as they idled on the runway. They were all lined up for take-off. Once inside the operations building Bonham met with Lieutenant Vera Brown. She and a medical technician were the other two members of her team. Outside, Bonham and Brown could see hundreds of soldiers waiting to board the other cargo planes. Forty-seven soldiers were already aboard Bonham's plane, a C-54. The cargo plane had been transformed into a miniature hospital emergency room.

Their normal routine was anything but normal. After the returning troops were unloaded, the wounded would be immediately loaded. Time was of the essence, because much of the time that they were flying into the landing zones, unloading troops, loading the wounded, and then taking off again, they were under heavy enemy fire. On this day things would be quite different.

Once Bonham and Brown had boarded their plane, the pilot told them to try to get some sleep. But neither was ready. They sat next to each other and talked as the big engines of the C-54 began to roar as they moved down the runway. The plane slowly began to climb into the air as it left the runway and went up over the shores of the Sea of Japan. When the plane was about a half mile from shore, it suddenly stalled and dropped from the sky. The C-54 slammed into the Sea of Japan. The impact made an awful noise and the whole aircraft began to submerge at once. The force of the crash caused the huge cargo plane to break into three pieces. Jonita Bonham found herself completely underwater and fought with all of her strength to reach the surface. Once she had made it and gasped her first breath of air, Jonita, in total darkness, listened as water began to swallow up the cargo plane.

Desperately she fought to keep herself above the water and to escape the confines of what was left of the aircraft. What made things worse was that the wind had whipped the sea into a churning mass of water. Kicking her legs with all of her might to keep afloat, Bonham was finally able to grab onto a floating barracks bag that came near her. Some of the men around her were swimming, while others "floated in the water terribly still." For the first half minute everything around her was very quiet. A voice out of the dark soon brought Jonita back to the world of sound. "There's a life raft here," a man shouted. "How do you inflate it?" Without hesitation Jonita yelled back, "Yank it out of its case and it will inflate itself!" Then she took command of the situation. The pilot and co-pilot were both dead and Vera Brown had vanished.

In the next moment, Bonham saw the silhouette of the raft bounce high on a wave. She let go of the barracks bag and began to swim towards the raft, as did about a half dozen men. One of the men close by saw Jonita and screamed to the others, "Here's one of the nurses!"

She felt an arm pushing her towards the raft. Once she reached the raft, she grabbed the rope that trailed from the vessel and then chose to stay in the water. Jonita shook the water from her face and eyes and began looking for others who were still in the water. She could see the surface of the waters spotted with the heads of swimming men. Bonham then reached out to the closest man and grabbed him and guided his fingers towards the life rope. Then she found another and then another until she had seventeen men with her. All were able to get onto the raft, except Jonita. In the darkness, she could make out another life raft about twenty yards away and saw men getting into it. Once Jonita was sure that everyone who had survived was on the life rafts, she allowed some of the men to reach down into the cold churning waters and drag her up over the side.

Once she lay back in the crowded raft, the pain hit her like a large hammer. Her head and chest throbbed as a wave of nausea hit her. Bonham's left arm hurt and as she held it up, she could see that her wrist was bent to one side. She knew it was broken, but she didn't have time to worry about it. She was responsible for the lives of the survivors in the two rafts and she didn't know how long it would be before help arrived.

One man in the raft panicked and shouted that he was going to swim for it, but Bonham commanded him to stay on the raft: "This water is full of sharks. Besides you'd be blown out to sea in this weather. Take it easy, soldier. Rescue boats will be here in a minute, now."

Ironically, no one at base operations knew the C-54 had crashed. As the life rafts floated, Bonham and the others could see the other planes taking off from the airstrip, but none of the planes could see through the darkness to the Sea of Japan's surface.

Many of the seventeen men with her were seriously injured. In rough seas and with water pouring into the two rafts, it was impossible for Bonham to give first aid. What she could do though was comfort them and keep the other survivors busy by shouting orders to them. Forgetting her own injuries, she talked panicked men out of jumping into the water and kept encouraging them to stay calm until her throat was raw. After they had been in the water for a couple of hours, one of the men saw a light. Sure enough, there was a light, and its reflection cut across the water's surface.

"Start yelling!" Bonham ordered. "Everybody yell!" she again commanded. "All together! Everybody on both rafts! Keep on yelling!" She knew that there was a slim chance they would be heard above the sea's waves and the wind. The light vanished for a moment, then reappeared. Those who could shout continued to do so as their voices rolled on through the darkness and over the watery abyss below them. Little by little the craft with the light came nearer. Jonita could make out its form as it approached. It was a Japanese fishing vessel. As the boat approached, some of the men in the raft began to scramble up, ready to leap to safety, but again Bonham's voice rang through the air with a command. "Stay where you are! You'll capsize us. Here, pass this line to them. Show them the other raft. Have them tow us ashore … both rafts."

Once she saw that both rafts were secured to the fishing boats and felt the jerk of the lines, Bonham was able to relax a little. Everything went dim for her, but she was not unconscious. The last thing she remembered was reaching shore. The next thing she saw was the inside of the hospital. And that's all she would see for the next nine months.

Jonita Bonham's injuries were very extensive, including a broken cheekbone. When it was discovered she needed more than just one surgery on her head, she was eventually transferred to Maxwell Air Force Base Hospital in Alabama. By this time the news had already been telling Jonita's life story all over the United States. How she was born and raised in Oklahoma City, Oklahoma, and went to nursing school there. How she enlisted in what was then called the Army Air Corps and commissioned as a 2nd Lieutenant in the Medical Corps during World War II. And how she stayed in the Philippines and Japan just after the war ended. She left the military for a short time and when the war in Korea broke out, she had no hesitation in volunteering her services again. She was now a 1st Lieutenant and her face was seen around the nation.

One day, after she had undergone her third head surgery, Jonita Bonham was notified that Lieutenant General George Stratemeyer was coming for a visit. This really bothered her because she didn't have any hair. It had all been shaved off because of her surgery. A friend found a nice scarf that could be tied around her head. Jonita couldn't for the life of her think why a general would want to see her. If she hadn't been so incapacitated with her shoulder and arm cast, Jonita would have fallen out of the bed she was in when she found out the reason for his visit. General Stratemeyer presented Jonita Bonham with the Distinguished Flying Cross, the highest decoration for valor that the Air Force bestows. Had Bonham been in Korea when the crash occurred, she probably would have been given the Congressional Medal of Honor, but she would have had to been in a combat zone to be eligible for that decoration. As it was, Jonita in her hospital bed had the DFC pinned on her pajamas by General Stratemeyer. This made Jonita Ruth Bonham the only woman in the history of the Korean War to be the recipient of the Air Force's highest award for valor!

Once the news media got hold of this story and photo (taken at the time of the ceremony in the hospital), America had a new, genuine hero. Newspapers and magazines plastered their covers with her face. *Everywoman's Magazine* and *Reader's Digest* both ran stories about Bonham. Then on April 9, 1952, The Cavalcade of America radio program aired her story. It starred the movie actress Nina Foch as Jonita (who was called Bonnie in those days). Millions of Americans heard her story and later a movie, *Flight Nurse,* was made about Jonita's experiences. Jonita didn't like to brag about anything she accomplished. She didn't allow the Hollywood hype to affect her demeanor.

Shortly after her being presented with the DFC, Jonita Bonham was promoted to captain, but she married a major, Major Clifford Boveé, the medical officer who was with her shortly after her crash and the same man who wrote the letter to her parents.

Bonham's injuries caused her considerable pain for some time and the Air Force eventually gave her a full medical retirement from the service. For years after, while raising her family, she traveled the world with her husband Cliff, who remained in the military. They finally retired to Colorado Springs, Colorado.

On December 24, 1994 Jonita Ruth Bonham-Boveé quietly passed away from an insidious killer, cancer, in the home of her daughter Renee. Her story, like all heroes' stories, has faded in the minds of all except those whom she saved and those who loved her. She was a gentle and fun-loving woman and she returned to flying. Jonita Bonham loved her family and enjoyed her special friends, but although she enjoyed the beauty of the ocean, she never again ventured into its waters.

20

Jóse Marti

His Eloquence Is Still Heard

Any American who listened to pop radio in the summer of 1966 heard Jóse Marti's words three to four times a day and yet had no idea who he was. Unless you were Cuban or Cuban American. The words (sung badly in Spanish by the American group The Sandpipers) and the music to this song became a huge hit. The best part of the song was when the words were translated and spoken in English while a soprano backup singer continued to sing beautifully in Spanish. The name of the song was "Guantanamera," and it was the number 9 song on the "top forty" charts for weeks. All who listened to the words were struck by the eloquence and poignancy that came over the airways:

> I am a sincere man from
> the land of the palm trees.
> Before dying, I wish to
> pour forth the poems of my soul.
>
> My verses are soft green,
> but they are also flaming red.
> My verses are like
> wounded fauns seeking
> refuge in the forest

I want to share my fate
with the world's humble.
A little mountain stream
pleases me more than the ocean."

The music to the song was copyrighted in 1965, but the poem was written by Jóse Marti in 1882. Marti was one of Cuba's most brilliant writers and is still called the "Father of Free Cuba." His name and words are revered, not only by the anti-communist Cubans, but also by Fidel Castro himself. The name Marti still stands as a symbol of all that is great in men and what they are willing to sacrifice for freedom. And as in the case of many great men, Jóse Marti had a very humble beginning.

Jóse Marti y Perez was born in Havana, Cuba, on January 28, 1853. Both of his parents had been born in Spain. By all accounts, Jóse's mother was a gentle woman, but his father was a sergeant in the Spanish army that occupied Cuba. He was an authoritarian who demanded unquestioning obedience from his family. He in turn gave his obedience to the army of Spain. No matter how many injustices were heaped upon the Creoles and Afro-Cubans who populated Cuba, Sergeant Mariano Marti showed no signs of compassion. This lack of feeling became a source of resentment to the compassionate and equally strong minded Jóse. As he grew older and watched the atrocities Spain committed upon the Cuban people, Jóse's resentment towards his father turned to alienation.

All of this started when Jóse was nine years old. His father was transferred to the small town of Hanabana, in eastern Cuba. It was here that young Jóse first witnessed the incredible cruelties to the black slaves in that town. It changed him forever. He watched as many of the slaves there were viciously whipped and beaten by the Spanish. Later in his life he wrote: "And the blacks? Who has ever seen a friend physically whipped and does not consider himself forever in his debt? I saw it, I saw it when I was a child, and I can still feel the shame burning on my cheeks."

Jóse's mother Leonor became very concerned about her son's exposure to these atrocities. Leonor finally talked her husband into letting her take Jóse back to Havana, where she enrolled him in school at the prestigious Escuela Superior Municipal de Verones (the Municipal Senior Boys' School). The school and its director, Rafael Maria den Mendive, a well-known Cuban poet, had an incredible impact on young Jóse. During this time Mendive was considered Cuba's greatest poet and a man of letters. This great intellect was the exact opposite of Sergeant Mariano Marti. Mendive was kind, articulate, and intelligent. He spoke of philosophy and poets, while Jóse's father thought an education was a waste of time. Boys Jóse's age, he told his wife, should be working, not reading. But in what seemed a cruel world, established by Spain's colonization of Cuba, Jóse found hope and comfort in the words and ways of Mendive. He became a frequent and welcome visitor at Mendive's home. Here, he learned more of poetry, philosophy, social reform, and politics.

Jóse Marti dared to dream and think that Cuba could and should one day be free to rule itself, and that everyone should be equal. In October 1868, Marti saw that his dream might be within sight when he received his initial exposure to Cuban politics. When Cuba's First War of Independence broke out, Marti and other young thinkers began meeting at Mendive's home for discussions and poetry readings about their thoughts of a possibly free Cuba. By the beginning of 1869 Jóse Marti was convinced that Cuba should be free and that he would be more than just an observer of the events taking place around him.

Marti and another student began publishing periodicals strongly critical of Spain's policies in Cuba. *El Diablo Cojuelo* (*The Limping Devil*) and *La Patria Libre* (*The Free Motherland*) were published by Marti, with Mendive's financial backing. The effect was incredible. Spain considered these publications extremely dangerous and thought that Mendive was the writer. The Spanish government arrested and exiled Mendive, who in turn never let them know the words were Marti's.

After Mendive's arrest and exile, Jóse Marti was finally arrested and tried for treason. He was found guilty, and the seventeen year old was sentenced to six years' hard labor in a Cuban work camp. From dawn until sunset, Marti and other prisoners worked breaking rocks in a government quarry. Marti's legs were shackled with irons during his six-month ordeal. He was finally released, through the intervention of his father's well-connected friends. When Marti walked out of the prison, he was almost blind because of his work in the tropical sun and his ankles were permanently scarred from his shackles, but his views about Spanish rule were unchanged. Of his six months in prison he later wrote, "These pages should be known by no other name but infinite pain.

"Infinite pain, for the pain of prison is the harshest, the most devastating of afflictions, that which kills the intelligence and withers the soul, leaving effects that will never be erased.

"It begins with a length of iron chain; it drags with it this mysterious world that troubles the heart; it grows, nourished upon every somber sorrow, and finally wanders about magnified by every scalding tear."

Within weeks, Marti was exiled to Spain by the Spanish government. They felt he could not cause any more trouble so far from Cuba. They were wrong.

Marti began publishing articles about the cruel treatment of Cuban political prisoners by the Spanish government. Then he enrolled at Madrid's Central University, where he studied law, philosophy, and literature. Frequently, he would journey into the Spanish Cortes, the Spanish legislature, and watch the proceedings. He was fascinated with its process. He also knew that knowledge of your enemy's laws and how they enact them is a requisite if you want to challenge them.

While in Spain, young Marti became famous among the Cuban exiles and immigrants for his writings and speeches. He became a much-sought-after lecturer at universities throughout Madrid and Barcelona, but he was still a defiant man in exile. Marti was in Spain in 1873 when the Cortes successfully repulsed the King's artillery corps that had been sent to disperse them. And they successfully forced the King of Spain to abdicate. Spain had declared herself a republic, but she would not free the colony of Cuba.

Marti was deeply disappointed that the new republic had no intention of freeing his homeland. He delivered a passionate essay entitled "The Spanish Republic and the Cuban Revolution" to Estanisloa Figueras, the head of the republic. His brilliant oration during a meeting with the republic leaders fell on deaf ears. Outraged by this indifference, Marti moved to northern Spain, where he immersed himself in his studies. On June 25, 1874, he earned a bachelor's degree. One week later he passed his master's exam in law and then excelled in passing in the Faculty of Philosophy and Letters. He received his master's degree in that department for his thesis on the Roman philosopher Cicero. Within the year, Spain broke out in revolution again, the Republic was overthrown, and the monarchy was reinstated.

Marti wanted to leave Spain. Although he was not allowed to returned to Cuba, he could go to other colonies, such as Mexico. In January 1875, Jóse Marti moved to Mexico. After a death in his family he was reunited with them for the first time in four years. His father forgave him his treason to his mother country and was proud of his academic achievements. In fact, Marti no longer resented his father. In a letter to his sister Amelia, Jóse wrote of their father, "You don't know just how much tender respect and veneration our father warrants. While at first he may appear full of grumpiness and silly notions, in fact he's a man with extraordinary virtue. Now that I'm an adult, I can appreciate the value of his energy, as well as the rare, sublime merit of his pure, forthright nature." Jóse was finally able to accept his father for who he was and not what he did for a living.

Over the next two years, Marti traveled throughout Guatemala and Mexico and at one point sneaked back into Cuba under an assumed name, but only briefly. In 1877, in Mexico, he married Carmen Zayas Bazan, the beautiful daughter of a Cuban immigrant. He took his new bride back to Guatemala, where he took a teaching position. Although his new married life brought Marti peace, there was still something missing, his home, Cuba! Also in 1877, Marti began writing again about how all of the Latin American countries and their problems were different from those of Spain and each other. Within a year, he and his wife were allowed to return to Cuba.

Being home brought out more of Marti's desire for Cuba to be free, but he was not allowed to be a member of the revolutionary council. His words, both spoken and written, challenged the council's leaders, because they were military men. After his years of exile in Spain and Mexico, Marti was quick to remember that the revolutionary military leaders in those countries all chose to become dictators when the fighting was over. In 1879, after a failed "Little War" for independence, Marti was again arrested and exiled to Spain. He didn't stay long this time, traveling to France and then to the United States. In 1884 he was named consul of Uruguay.

In the following years, Marti continually wrote and organized movements against Spain's continued hold on Cuba. He solicited money and manpower throughout parts of the United States, Cuba, and other Latin American countries. He particularly spent time in New York City, Tampa, and Key West, where there were large concentrations of the Cuban population working in cigar factories.

By 1892, plans for the second Cuban revolution were truly underway, with Marti as one of the key planners. He began the publication *Patria* and was elected to the Cuban Revolutionary Party. He left Cuba for a short while to travel to the Dominican Republic to meet with the party's military leader, Maximo Gomez. During the next two years, Marti traveled extensively throughout Cuban communities in Latin America, meeting with exiled or hiding members of the revolutionary party. Their talks were always plans on how they could overthrow the Spanish government. Marti knew that there would be a lot of talking, writing, and dying for all who participated.

Marti was also a diplomat. In 1894, he traveled to Key West to help settle a labor dispute between Spanish tobacco plant owners and striking Cuban workers. He was so successful in helping the striking workers that they vowed to donate 25 cents a week to help finance the revolution. That 25 cents was equal to one day's wages. Their families would tighten their belts so that Cuba might be free, especially for Marti, who was now named the revolution's supreme leader.

One year later, when the shooting part of the revolution finally began, Major General Jóse Marti traveled to the front lines of Cuba by secreting himself aboard the German freighter Nordstand. Marti bribed the freighter's captain, who was on his way to Haiti from the Dominican Republic, with $1,000, to drop him and some of his followers off the coast of Cuba.

On April 10, 1895, the freighter set Marti and the others in a small rowboat, three miles off the coast of Oriental Province. It was a miracle that they reached Cuba at all. In his diary later that night Marti wrote:

> They lower the boat. Heavy downpour as we push off. Set the wrong course. Confused and conflicting opinions in the boat. Another downpour. Rudder lost. Back on course. I take forward oar. Salas rows steadily. Paquito Borrero and the General help out in the stern. We strap on our revolvers. Head toward clearing. Moon comes up red from behind a cloud. We land on a stony beach, La Playita (at the foot of Cabobaja). I the last to leave the boat, bailing it out. Jump ashore. Great joy!

Once ashore, they set up camp for the night. Six weeks prior to this landing, a general uprising had begun in the town of Baire, and now with the arrival of Marti and General Gomez, the hero of the First (failed) War of Independence, the Cuban people seemed ready to oust Spain from Cuba.

Early the next morning Marti and the others began their journey inland to meet with about 340 revolutionary soldiers. They settled in the jungles in the Guantanamo area of Cuba. On May 19, 1895, scouts reported that gunfire could be heard near Dos Rios (Two Rivers). Marti and Gomez did not know that they had been betrayed by two of their own. Thinking they could surprise the Spanish, they now found themselves in the middle of an intense fight with a superior force. Although ordered to stay out of harm's way by General Gomez, Jóse Marti could not bear to be left out of the fight. Astride a beautiful white stallion, he rode to the front. Within the blink of an eye, a Spanish trooper shot and mortally wounded Jóse Marti. Not knowing who he was, the Spanish buried his body in a crude casket in an unmarked grave. But when they found out later the next day that they had killed Marti, they dug up his grave, embalmed his body, and brought it to Havana for a huge public funeral. This was done to dishearten the people of Cuba. It did not work.

The patriots quickly reorganized and used Marti as their martyr. In the following year, although the revolutionaries were outnumbered, the fighting began taking its toll on Spain. There were now 200,000 Spanish troops fighting 50,000 rebels. Morale was low in the Spanish army, but it was contagiously high among the rebels, who enjoyed the support of the people in the countryside. The entire island of Cuban was under control of the revolutionary army, with the exception of the large cities, including Havana.

Tomas Estrada Palma replaced Marti as the leader of the Cuban Revolutionary Party. His relationship with General Gomez and others became strained after awhile. Palma thought that the rebels should court aid from the United States in the form of arms, ammunition, and soldiers. The military leaders, however, only wanted weapons. They did not want foreign soldiers. Palma argued that with U.S. help the war would be quickly won. He was right. Although the United States did not want to take an active role in the fighting, an event that occurred on February 15, 1898, changed the situation. The battleship *Maine* was blown up in Havana harbor, killing 260 U.S. sailors. This incident (which was later found out to have been caused by faulty ammunition on the ship, not sabotage) brought the United States into Cuba's affairs and the Spanish American War had begun for this country. The fighting, though harsh and bloody, only lasted three months.

The United States firmly entrenched itself in Cuba. Her natural resources would be great for American business and through a series of treaties, Cuba lost her ability to control her own foreign relations. The U.S. military would ensure that. The United States Navy established a base in Guantanamo. It is still operating there. Cuba was now free, but she really wasn't. Her freedom didn't arrive until many years later, and then it was taken away again.

In the 1930s General Fulgencio Batista overthrew the Cuban government and proclaimed himself dictator. He ruled for over ten years and then was forced from power. In 1952, however, Batista again overthrew the government and opened Cuba's doors wide to American business. People like gangsters Lucky Luciano and Sam Giancana helped set up the gambling casinos that made Havana famous during those years. Any old-time sailor will tell you that Havana was the greatest liberty port in the world. There were shows, gambling, and all the liquor one could drink. Batista became rich. If you were to do business in Cuba, you did business with Batista. While this went on in the city, the people of the countryside suffered. Secret police watched what everyone did, and sometimes people would disappear.

During this period a young scholar started a rebel army. He was a student of Marti's words and life, and he would use Marti's name to help his rebellion. His name was Fidel Castro. In January 1959, after five years of fighting, Castro triumphantly marched into Havana, while Batista and the Americans caught in the fight all fled Cuba. There were many executions of those in Batista's army who did not escape and what Jóse Marti had feared most happened: A military leader who had fought for the freedom of his country turned dictator!

Ironically, Castro's victory spawned a new interest in Marti and his works. Marti's works had been all but forgotten during the Batista era. Castro renamed Havana's busiest thoroughfare Marti Boulevard, and the national airport, the main library, and the central plaza were all named for Marti also. But Castro wasn't the only one using Marti's name for his own purposes.

Exiled Cubans in Miami, Florida, with the help of the U.S. government, to this day make daily radio broadcasts to Cuba via "Radio Marti."

The legacy of Jóse Marti is not that of politicians, dictators, or non-Latin American governments. Marti's legacy is the principles he defined and defended throughout his life, which eventually ended his life: individual liberty and national self-determination. He was a man who devoted himself to his people and ridding his country of imperial domination. He stood firmly on the side of the weak, the poor, and the minorities of his country. He abhorred slavery and those who profited from the suffering of others; be they slavers or big business owners who abused their workers. Marti's writings are incredibly stirring, thought provoking, and poignant. Yet he is almost unknown in non-Cuban circles.

Jóse Marti's books and poetry can still be found in bookstores in "Little Havana" in Miami, Florida, and in some public libraries. Or, if, once in awhile, you're listening to a "golden oldie" radio station, you may hear a song sung badly in Spanish, but when the song is translated into English, you will hear Marti's words, "I am a sincere man from the land of the palm trees. ... Before dying, I wish to pour forth the poems of my soul."

Quotes from Jóse Marti

1. "Barricades of ideas are worth more than barricades of stone."

    "There is no prow that can cut through a cloudbank of ideas. A powerful idea, waved before the world at the proper time, can stop a squadron of iron-clad ships, like the mystical flag of the Last Judgement."

2. "The thought is the father to the deed."

3. [*Author's note: After living in the United States for almost two years, Jóse Marti was convinced that, because of their very different origins, Latin America should avoid being influenced by North America.*]

    "There are avaricious races like that of the North whose formidable hunger requires virgin people. And there are faithful races like that of the South whose offspring want no other sun to warm them than that of their patria and who desire no other riches than the golden orange and the white lily grown in their grandparent's garden."

4.   "I adore simplicity, but not that simplicity which comes from limiting my ideas to this or that circle or school. Rather I prefer the type of simplicity to say what I see, feel, or think with the least number of words possible—using words that are powerful, graphic, energetic, and harmonious."

5.

In the nation beloved by me
I would like to see born
The nation that can be
Without hate, and without color.
In the generous game
Of limitless thought.
I would like to see building the house,
Rich and poor, black and white.

21

Daisy Anderson

"I Just Want People to Get Along with Each Other"

Author's note: I only met Daisy once and our conversation lasted only about two hours. I had planned to visit her again in the Amberwood Court Care Center in Denver, but she passed away before I could return. Her death was a great loss for anyone who ever met this remarkable woman. A teacher friend of mine said that Daisy would come into her school and talk to the children about her life as the last "Civil War Widow" and all the other things she did in her ninety-seven years. So, I made the journey out to her care center on East Asbury Street and introduced myself to this incredible lady. In the course of our conversation, Daisy told me that she had lived in Forest City, Arkansas, for a number of years. It was there, she said, that she had met her husband in 1921. I told her that I knew that city well, as I travel through there twice a year, on Interstate 40, on my way to Tennessee and the Carolinas. This November when I return to the Carolinas, I know that I won't be able to pass through Forest City, Arkansas, without thinking of Daisy.

What follows is a brief story of someone who overcame adversity in one of its ugliest forms: racism.

Daisy Anderson was born both poor and black on December 14, 1900, in Hardin County, Tennessee. Hardin County was a hard place to live in if you were black. The Ku Klux Klan still ruled the Tennessee countryside where it had been born only thirty-five years earlier. Former Confederate General Nathan Bedford Forrest was one of its founders. Forrest was known for his hatred of blacks whom he considered an inferior race. During the war, it was his Tennessee troops who, after storming Fort Pillow on the Mississippi River, lynched dozens of the black Union soldiers who had surrendered.

In 1900, hatred and racism still ran deep in the Tennessee countryside. For seventeen years Daisy and her family persevered, until it became too dangerous to live there. They moved to Forest City, Arkansas. There, Daisy's father worked as a sharecropper and she, along with her mother and siblings, picked cotton to help support the family. Later, Daisy put what little education she possessed to use, earning $10 a month teaching the alphabet to black children. Unlike many in her community, Daisy had completed the equivalent of an eighth-grade education.

Four years after her arrival in Arkansas, Daisy's minister arranged a meeting with a man who would become her husband. The meeting went well, but she never expected it to take the turn that it did. Daisy was only twenty-one and Robert Ball Anderson was seventy-nine! He was old enough to be her grandfather! During that first year, Daisy grew to love this elderly man for his extreme kindness and his generosity to her family.

Robert Ball Anderson had lived an incredible life and now wanted to share it with Daisy. A former slave from Greensburg, Kentucky, he ran away from his owners and joined the Union Army in early 1865. He enlisted with the 125th United States Colored Troops. The plains Indians they fought called them "Buffalo Soldiers." Anderson was discharged in Missouri in 1867. From Missouri he traveled to Iowa where he dabbled in land, but con men and grasshoppers forced him to move to Nebraska. There he bought a homestead and invested in real estate and diamonds. What happened next was almost impossible for an ex-slave. He became independently wealthy!

While visiting Arkansas on that fateful day in 1922, Anderson met Daisy. Over the next few weeks the elderly Anderson courted Daisy. She later said that she was so poor when they met, "I didn't have a chair to sit on or a table to sit at."

They were married on March 19, 1922, in Forest City, Arkansas. It was the first and only marriage for both Robert and Daisy. Daisy once commented, "I was an old man's darling. I tell you he spoiled me for the rest of my life!" They journeyed to Colorado Springs, Colorado, for their honeymoon and then settled on Robert's 2,000 acre ranch near Hemingford, Nebraska.

Their marriage was a happy one for the eight and a half years they were together. Three years before Robert's death on November 30, 1930, in an automobile accident, Daisy Anderson published a book about her husband's remarkable life. The book, *From Slavery to Affluence: Memoirs of Robert Anderson, Ex-Slave,* told of Robert's slave experiences, his days as a "Buffalo Soldier," and later his life as an emancipated adult.

After Robert's death, Daisy Anderson headed for South Dakota and lived there until 1937. From there she moved to Colorado to join her sister and brother, who were living in Steamboat Springs. They were the only blacks living there. None of the whites wanted them. They lived in an area called Strawberry Park. Although at first they lived on the money Daisy had inherited from Robert, eventually they had to earn more, and began growing strawberries from seeds Daisy's brother found. Nobody would sell them any plants. But Mother Nature and Daisy's green thumb, "made them little plants bloom until they were full of strawberries." Within the next few years, Daisy Anderson had eight acres of strawberries and raspberries and hundreds of chickens. She also had cabins built that she rented out to hunters, hiring herself out as their guide in the rugged Colorado wilderness.

She worked for herself and always kept herself busy, well into this century, when age finally slowed her body down. She was a poet and lecturer and often spoke at schools, always teaching tolerance.

Daisy Anderson finally was moved into a nursing home in 1991 at the age of ninety-one. But she was determined to remain active spending time with children and visitors like myself. One of the highlights of Daisy Anderson's incredible life occurred in 1997. She was visited by the president of the United States, Bill Clinton. She presented him with a bouquet of flowers and an autographed copy of her book. When he left her only comment was, "Wow. Isn't that something."

Daisy died peacefully on September 20, 1998, at the care center. On October 17, 1998, she was posthumously inducted into the Arkansas Black Hall of Fame. Daisy Anderson lived a full and long life. Her legacy is one of tolerance and forgiveness. All she ever wanted was for "people to learn to get along with each other."

22

Dr. Victor Westphall and Angel Fire

In a quiet place on a sacred hill
Where spirits come to rest.
Beyond a pass called Cimmaron
Two thousand miles to the west
Of a black granite wall there stands a holy spire
To honor those who died in 'Nam
And they call it Angel Fire.

In the Moreno Valley of northern New Mexico, just outside the town of Angel Fire, there stands a memorial to those men and women who died in the Vietnam War. What is unique about this memorial is that it was built eleven years before the National Vietnam Memorial in Washington, D.C., called "The Wall."

It was built out of the love of a father for his son, who was killed in that war. And yet this love was not a selfish love. It was extended to all those men and women who served in that war: the living, the dead, and those who were maimed in body and spirit. And to all non-veterans who visit this remarkable place, the spirits of old still seem to dwell here.

From the time man first walked this valley to this day, strange and unusual incidents, as though guided by those spirits, have occurred frequently. In the early days of the eighteenth century the Utah Indians (the Utes) first reported to the Catholic priests there that the valley was a sacred resting place for warriors. They told the priests, who were there to convert the Utes to Catholicism, that there was a fire that appeared in autumn's and winter's early morning skies above Agua Fria (Cold Water) Peak. Red and bright orange colors wove their hues into morning's blue and grey cloak that sheltered the mountaintop. The Utes told the priests that it was in fact the fire of the gods that visited the land. The priests, while trying to gently coax these native people into their realm of Christianity, told the Utes there was only one god, and that he had helpers called angels. From that time on this area of New Mexico was called "El Fuego de Los Angeles" or Angel Fire.

Over the past thirty years, however, many unexplained events have occurred in this ancient resting place for warriors. These events began on May 27, 1968. While clearing land with a backhoe on a hilltop just outside the town of Angel Fire, Dr. Victor Westphall was concentrating so hard on his task that he didn't notice the government car that drove up to where he was working. He did notice two men get out of the car and call out his name. The two men were dressed in Marine Corps uniforms and wore the rank of captain on their collars and epaulets. They had come on the dreaded job of delivering the message no parent wants to hear.

Dr. Westphall turned off the backhoe's engine and stared at the two men. Horror filled his entire being. There could be only one reason these men were here. The leader of the two men asked, "Are you Doctor Victor Westphall?"

Almost numb, Doctor Westphall replied that he was in fact the person for whom they were looking. Then he heard the words, "Your son has been killed." An uneasy silence followed. "David?" he softly asked. The two captains looked at each other as though they had just made a huge blunder.

"No sir, your son Victor," the leader said. It was then that realization sank in for Dr. Westphall. David and Victor were the same person. He and his wife had named their oldest son Victor David Westphall III, but called him David.

After Dr. Westphall had cleared up the confusion, the two captains asked if there was anything they could do for him, but of course there really wasn't. The two captains informed Dr. Westphall that David was killed in action in the vicinity of Quang Tri, Republic of South Vietnam on May 22, 1968. There was little more information they could give him. The two uniformed men then departed, leaving Dr. Westphall alone with his grief. Time seemed to stop for this man who held a Ph.D. in philosophy; at this moment no words or great sayings could comfort him. Now it was his turn to be the messenger to his wife.

And the fire of the gods appeared
To fulfill one man's desire
That his son and all who died in 'Nam
Rest in peace in Angel Fire

Within weeks of David's tragic death, Dr. Westphall began having dreams about his oldest son. Some showed David lying down where the left side of his face could not be seen and in others his son appeared to him to talk. Victor Westphall felt as if there was something his son was trying to tell him. As though compelled by the ancient spirits of the valley and his son David, Victor Westphall decided to build a memorial. And he would build it on the land on which his son last lived before going into the Marine Corps.

Dr. Westphall hired an architect from Santa Fe to design something different. The building should not only be appropriate for a memorial chapel, but should also reflect the spirit of the valley, to honor those who died in that far-away land. What evolved was a white three-sided building that curved and spired towards the sky. It was completely hand stuccoed. But the building of this memorial was not to be completed without opposition.

1968 was the "Year of the Monkey" in Vietnam, but here in the United States the "Age of Aquarius" was being born. Both Martin Luther King Jr. and Robert Kennedy were slain, and President Lyndon B. Johnson chose not to run for re-election as the anti-war movement reached its peak. With the anti-war movement came a resentment towards anyone who served in uniform, let alone anyone who would build a memorial to the dead. In this "Year of the Monkey" the two most hated things in America were Vietnam veterans and police. The police brutality in Chicago during the Democratic National Convention didn't help change the public's perception.

Many of Moreno Valley's citizens were opposed to Dr. Westphall's plan, but he persevered for three years, having built much of the memorial chapel with his own two hands. A thirteen-foot cross was placed in the chapel where two of the three sides come together. Unbeknownst to Dr. Westphall at that time, the number thirteen had an incredible significance. He later found out that David was one of thirteen men who were killed in that ambush. This was only the first of many "coincidences" to occur.

The Vietnam Memorial at Angel Fire was dedicated on November 11, 1971, eleven years before the "The Wall" in Washington, D.C. Dr. Victor Westphall financed this project with his own money and opened the doors to all veterans of Vietnam and visitors. Not long after, veterans began coming to this ancient valley. Word had gotten out that someone had built a place for the veterans who were not allowed to tell their stories to the American public. Memorial Day was the time for the largest gathering of these men whom the public had shunned.

Thousands of vets from all walks of life arrived just to be in a place where they were welcome, where they could grieve and try to find some peace. Word had definitely gotten out.

When the "first" National Vietnam Memorial, "The Wall," was dedicated in 1982, it received an incredible amount of publicity and fanfare, and yet the Angel Fire memorial was a national secret, except from the Vietnam veterans. Many vets journeyed to Washington, D.C. to find the names of the dead carved onto the black granite wall, and then on to Angel Fire. It is here that they have felt the spirits of their dead comrades come to them.

In 1983, the Disabled American Veterans (the DAV) entered into an agreement with Dr. Westphall. They would build a visitor's center and request federal recognition for his memorial as "the second National Vietnam Memorial" if Dr. Westphall would deed the property over to the DAV. He would stay on the property as the executive manager. They would also build an apartment and office for him. The DAV in turn would build the visitor's center and hire an operating manager to run the everyday business.

In 1984, the visitor's center was complete and the DAV National Memorial was dedicated. The following year thousands of Vietnam veterans gathered on what would turn out to be an incredible weekend. Veterans found friends they thought were dead, nurses found patients they had treated, and medivac (medical evacuation) pilots found people they had flown to hospitals. But the most incredible incident would happen on Memorial Day itself.

During the closing ceremonies, an Air National Guard Unit was supposed to make a fly over. They never showed up. What did happen is still talked about today. A lone bald eagle appeared out of the sky and swooped down towards the chapel. The eagle then circled the chapel's spire four times and then flew off, never to be seen again that day. I was one of over 2,000 people who witnessed this event. I also found a friend there whom I thought was dead.

Shortly after the chapel's completion in 1971, Dr. Westphall had to leave the property to go on an errand. He locked the chapel's doors. When he returned a few hours later, he found a piece of plywood with a note etched in it with a rock. It simply asked, "Why did you lock me out, when I so desperately needed to come in?" From that day on the chapel at Angel Fire has never been locked. It is open twenty-four hours a day, 365 days of the year. Although it was extensively vandalized once, Dr. Westphall has refused to lock those doors.

In 1993, at the age of eighty, Dr. Victor Westphall made a pilgrimage to Vietnam. He took a handful of dirt from Angel Fire with him. Two Vietnam vets accompanied him to a place called Con Thien. With the help of the Vietnamese government they were able to find the location where David was killed. It was here that Dr. Westphall placed his handful of dirt. Then he picked up a handful of Vietnamese dirt and placed it in the same plastic bag he'd just emptied. Dr. Westphall then asked one of his Vietnamese escorts, "What does Con Thien translate to in English?" He was not prepared for the answer. Con Thien means "a Place of the Angels!" And even more incredibly, if a straight line were drawn down the angle where the two roads join, where David was killed, the design it creates is almost identical to the design of the chapel at Angel Fire.

For the past thirty years, since the death of his oldest son, Dr. Victor Westphall has taught tolerance to all and has publicly spoken out against war and violence. Once a year, in May, for the past ten years, he has personally greeted two busloads of students from Denver area middle schools, who come to learn about the Vietnam War. He has also helped many veterans to find peace of mind and comfort in soul. I know. He has taught me to overcome my hatred and prejudice. And for the past thirteen years he has been my friend and mentor.

Author's note: The Vietnam Memorial at Angel Fire, New Mexico, is located on U.S. Highway 64 approximately an hour and a half west of Raton, New Mexico, beyond Cimmaron Pass. If one is in Taos, New Mexico, the memorial is about twenty miles east on the same highway, but it takes about an hour to drive because of the mountains.

References

Chapter 1, Mochi

Mendoza, Patrick M. *Song of Sorrow: Massacre at Sand Creek*. Denver, CO: Willow Wind Publishing Company, 1993.

Interviews

Sherman Goose, Arapaho, OK, 1990–1997.

Cleo Sipes, Clinton, OK, 1989–August 1997. Great-grandaughter of Mochi.

John Sipes, Jr., Clinton, OK, 1989–1997. Great-great grandson of Mochi.

Bertha Wilson, Clinton, OK, 1995–1997. The author's Cheyenne aunt.

Terry Wilson, Clinton, OK, 1987–1997. Great-grandson of Mochi.

Chapter 2, The Shadow on the Wall

Newspapers

Charlotte Observer, December 1880. Article titled "Hanged to Death."

Research Venues

The North Carolina State Archives, University of North Carolina Library.

U.S. Census Reports for 1880, Cleveland County, NC and Pulaski County, KY, 1850.

Interviews

Phillip Sill, Lake Lure, NC, 1977. He was the first to tell me the story.

Dozens of elderly residents of Rutherford County. With the exception of Sarah Walker, I did not record their names in 1977.

Chapter 3, The Medal and the Lady: The Mary Edwards Walker Story

Editors of the Boston Publishing Company. *Above and Beyond: A History of the Congressional Medal of Honor from the Civil War to Vietnam.* Boston: Boston Publishing Co., 1985.

Research Venues

The Public Relations Office: The Mary Edwards Walker Memorial Medical Center, Oswego, NY.

The Congressional Medal of Honor Museum, Chattanooga, TN.

Chapter 4, Nathan's Legacy

Interviews

Eddie Bohn, 1985. Close friend and sparring partner of Jack Dempsey. Mr. Bohn was also a former State Senator of Colorado and owner of the Pig and Whistle Restaurant that was located at the corner of W. Colfax Ave. and Wolf Street for over sixty years. Mr. Bohn was an incredible storyteller and collector. Inside the old Pig and Whistle was a museum of Jack Dempsey photos and memorabilia and some of the best barbecue in Colorado.

People in Burnsville, Yancy County, NC, 1977.

John Parris, 1977. Writer for *Asheville Citizen Times.*

Chapter 5, Mother Maggard

Interviews

Tom Noel, Ph.D., University of Colorado, Denver, 1991, 1992.

Chapter 6, Silas Soule: A Forgotten Hero of Sand Creek

Mendoza, Patrick M. *Song of Sorrow: Massacre at Sand Creek.* Denver, CO: Willow Wind Publishing Co., 1993.

Mendoza, Patrick M., Ann Strange Owl, and Nico Strange Owl. *Four Great Rivers to Cross.* Englewood, CO: Libraries Unlimited, Inc., 1998.

Miscellaneous

Soule, Silas. Letters to his mother and sister. Colorado Historic Society, Denver, Colorado.

U. S. Congressional and Military Hearings, Denver, CO and Washington, DC, Spring 1865.

Chapter 7, Theodosia: A Lady Lost

Interviews

The late Clark Wilcox of the Hermitage in Murrell's Inlet, SC, 1979, 1983, 1984. When I last interviewed him on videotape fourteen years ago, he was ninety-seven years old. He was a wonderful storyteller and historian of South Carolina's low country.

Judge Charles Wedbee, Greenville, NC, 1977–1983. Author of many books about the Outer Banks, and historian.

The good people at the South Carolina Historic Society and the North Carolina Historic Society, 1979.

The "Bankers" of the Outer Banks of NC, since the 1960s.

The historian at the Oaks Plantation, 1976, 1977, 1984. Joseph Alston and his son Aaron Burr Alston are buried there. The Oaks Plantation is part of the four south plantations that were made into Brook Green Gardens in the 1930s. It is located a few miles south of Myrtle Beach, SC on U.S. 17.

Places Visited

The Oaks Plantation.

Theodosia Alston's home, 94 Church St., Charleston, SC.

Cape Hatteras, NC on thirteen separate occasions.

Chapter 8, Jules Bledsoe: The Voice

Interviews

In 1990, I was commissioned by the city of Waco, Texas, to write a multicultural musical history of their city and county. I was introduced to the descendants of Jules Bledsoe. The information in this story came directly from them and supporting documentation in their possession.

Chapter 9, Charles Gates Dawes: He Won the Nobel Peace Prize and Wrote a Song That Went to the Top 40

DeGregorio, William A. *The Complete Book of Presidents*. New York: Dembner Books, 1984.

Edwards, Tommy. "All in the Game," 1957. Back cover of this album says song written by a vice-president, but does not name Dawes.

Places Visited

The Pioneer Park Museum, Cheyenne, WY.

Chapter 10, The Day Doris Miller Became a Man

Interviews

This story came from the descendants of Dorrie Miller and the documentation in their possession while I was in Waco, Texas, in 1990.

Miscellaneous

U.S. Naval Records of his actions against the Japanese on December 7, 1941. The Citation for the Navy Cross.

Chapter 11, Billie and Patches

Interviews

Alice Lee Main, Director of Arts for the City of Aurora, CO, 1989.
Mary Pierce of the Aurora History Museum, 1989.
Billie Preston, 1989–1997.

Chapter 12, Sam Antonio: The Last Acoma to Survive

Cave, Dorothy. *Beyond Courage: One Regiment against Japan, 1941–1945*. Las Cruces, NM: Yucca Tree Press, 1992.

Matson, Eva Jane. *It Tolled For New Mexico: New Mexicans Captured by the Japanese 1941–1945.* Las Cruces, NM: Yucca Tree Press, 1992.

Petak, Joseph A. *Never Plan Tomorrow.* Fullerton, CA: Aquataur Press, 1991.

Interviews

Sam Antonio, Grants, NM, 1995–1997.

Miscellaneous

DD214s, Citation for Bronze Star and Purple Heart.

Guided tours of Acoma Pueblo by Sam Antonio.

Chapter 13, Shoichi Yokoi: The Last Japanese Soldier

Newspapers

Reports by U.S. news media, January 24, 1972.

Obituary: *Rocky Mountain News,* September 25, 1997.

Interviews

Ernie and Bobby Novey, Denver, CO, December 1997.

Chapter 14, One Extraordinary Event: The Day They Hanged an Elephant

Newspaper accounts on file at Erwin, TN, Public Library.

Chapter 15, Governor Ralph Carr: A Man of Compassion

Interviews

Bob Carr, 1998. Adopted son of Ralph Carr.

Henry Lowenstein, Denver, CO, 1989, 1990–1998.

Tom Noel, Ph.D., University of Colorado, Denver, 1995.

The good folks at Sukura Square, The Japanese Cultural Center, Denver, CO, 1996.

Miscellaneous

Copies of his biography and of speeches he made were made available to me by the Colorado Historical Society, Denver, CO, September 1997.

Chapter 16, Jeannette Pickering Rankin: The Lady from Montana

Davidon, Sue. *A Heart in Politics: Jeannette Rankin and Patsy T. Mink.* Seattle, WA: Seal Press, 1994.

Engelbarts, Rudolf. *Women in the United States Congress, 1917–1972.* Littleton, CO: Libraries Unlimited, Inc., 1974.

Interviews

Elderly people who knew Jeannette Rankin, in and around Athens, GA, 1993.

Chapter 17, Villains: Lavinia Fisher

Martin, Margaret Rhett. *Charleston Ghosts.* Columbia, SC: University of South Carolina Press, 1963.

Wellman, Manly Wade. *Dead and Gone: Classic Crimes of North Carolina.* Chapel Hill, NC: The University of North Carolina Press, 1954.

Interviews

Bruce Barnes, son of "Machine Gun Kelly," television interview, Discovery Channel, November 1997.

The good people of the Charleston Historic Society, Charleston, SC.

Jack Leland, 1977–1997. Charleston newsman, writer, and columnist.

Sarah Walker of Rutherford County, NC, 1977–1997. She passed away in September 1997 at age 97. Many of my stories started with interviews with the people of North Carolina, like Mrs. Walker. She had a minimal education but she was incredibly wise. She was born before there were paved roads or automobiles in Rutherford County and before the Wright Brothers made their first flight, but she lived to watch man walk on the moon. I have known Mrs. Walker and her family for over twenty years. She was a constant in my life during the eight years I lived and worked in the Carolinas and was a wealth of information about the people of Rutherford, McDowell, and Cleveland counties in North Carolina.

Archie Wills, 1977–1998. Lifelong Charleston resident and amateur historian.

Chapter 18, Those Weren't Ladies, They Were Pirates: Anne Bonny and Mary Read

Lee, Robert E. *Blackbeard the Pirate: A Reappraising of His Life and Times.* Winston-Salem, NC: Blair Publishing Co., 1974.

Interviews

South Carolina Historic Society. Charleston, SC, 1981-1997.

Jack Leland, Charleston, SC, 1981–1997. Retired writer, historian, and columnist.

Chapter 19, Jonita

Miscellaneous

All of the information in this story, including the personal letters, came directly from my friend of ten years, Renee Boveé, Jonita's daughter, and the Performing Arts Director for the Wyoming Arts Council. Shortly after Jonita's death, Renee invited me to her house to talk. The talk became this story. Jonita's military decorations are still with the family, as is the Citation for the Distinguished Flying Cross. Dozens upon dozens of newspaper articles were shared with me, as were the *Reader's Digest* article and the original play that the Cavalcade of America aired on April 9, 1952.

I had talked with Renee many times during her mother's illness to offer her support, as I had lost my own mother to cancer. I am only sorry I never had a chance to meet Jonita in person, but through Renee she came to life for me through each talk, letter, and article.

Chapter 20, Jóse Marti: His Eloquence Is Still Heard

Kirk, John M. *Jose Marti: Mentor of the Cuban Nation.* Tampa, FL: University Presses of Florida, University of South Florida, 1983.

Marti, Jose. *Our America: Writings on Latin America and the Struggle for Cuban Independence.* New York: Monthly Review Press, 1977.

Interviews

Cuentos de mi Abuela—the stories my grandmother, Amparo Salinas Mendoza, told me. She was born in Havana, Cuba, in 1884, and came to the United States in 1898, during the revolution. She lived the remainder of her life in Key West, FL and died in 1968.

Cuentos de mi Padre—the stories my father told me.

Charles Gonzales Mendoza—writer and admirer of Marti's works. Born August 16, 1919 in Key West, FL. Died July 27, 1977 in Denver, CO.

Chapter 21, Daisy Anderson: "I Just Want People to Get Along with Each Other"

Newspapers

Rocky Mountain News, September 24, 1998, pp. 5A, 20A.

Interviews

Daisy Anderson, Denver, CO, May 1997.

Chapter 22, Doctor Victor Westphall and Angel Fire

Interviews

Michael Peters (USN retired), Angel Fire, NM, 1994–1998. Former manager at the Memorial. Peters and I both served on PBRs (Patrol Boat River) in the Mekong Delta, though not at the same time.

Victor Westphall and others, thirteen years of interviews and casual talks.

Miscellaneous

Personal observations of many of the events listed in the story.

Index

Abolitionists, 29
Acoma, 59–60, 65, 69
Adams, John, 52
African Americans
  Anderson, Daisy, 122–125
  Bledsoe, Jules, 44–45
  Carney, William H. (Sergeant), 20
  Chisholm, Shirley, 91
  Miller, Doris, 53–54
Alston, Joseph, 40, 42
Alston, Theodosia Burr, 39–43
Anderson, Daisy, 122–125
Anderson, Robert Ball, 123–124
Angel Fire, 126–131
Antonio, Sam, 59–70
Apache, 20
Arapaho, 5, 26–27, 31, 37
Arlington National Cemetery, 21
Arkansas Black Hall of Fame, 125

Barnes, Bruce Jr., 96
Barnes, Katherine, 96
Batista, Fulgencio, 118–119
Beckwourth, Jim, 35
Beecher, Henry Ward, 29
"Beecher's Bibles," 29
Bent, William, 32
Benevidez, Roy (Master Sergeant), 21
Black Kettle. See Moke Tavato
Blackbeard. See Teach, Edward
Bledsoe, Jules, 44–45
Bonham, Jonita, 102–110
Bonnet, Stede, 98
Bonny, Anne, 97–99
Bonny, James, 98
Booth, John Wilkes, 38
Boveé, Clifford, 103, 109
Breckinridge, John Cabell, 50
Bronze Star Medal, 69
Brown, John, 29
Brown, Vera, 103, 105–106
Buchanan, James, 50
Buffalo Soldiers, 123–124
Bureau of Indian Affairs, 60, 86

Burnsides, Ambrose (Major General), 15
Burr, Aaron, 39, 40, 43

"Calico Jack." See Rackham, Jack
Cape Hatteras, 39, 41, 42
Capone, Al, 46, 48
Carney, Sergeant William H., 20
Carr, Ralph, 78–83
Castro, Fidel, 112, 119
Charlotte Observer, 13
Cherokee, 51, 56, 57
Cheyenne, 1–6, 20, 31, 32, 33, 37
Chisholm, Shirley, 91
Chivington, John Milton (Colonel), 1, 4, 30–37
Civil Rights Movement, 91
Civil War, 10, 15–16, 19, 20, 28–29, 46, 122
Cleveland, Grover, 50, 51
Clinton, William (Bill), 125
Cody, Buffalo Bill, 20
Colley, Samuel, 31
Confederacy. See Civil War
Confederate Army. See Civil War
Congressional Medal of Honor, 17, 18, 19, 54, 109
Coolidge, Calvin, 47, 48
Crook, George (Lieutenant Colonel), 20
Cuban Revolutionary Party, 116, 118
Custer, George Armstrong, 19, 47
Custer, Tom, 19

Darlington Agency, 7
Dawes, Charles Gates, 46–49
Dempsey, Hirum, 23–24
Dempsey, Nathan, 22–24
Dempsey, William Harrison (Jack), 24–25
Denver Post, 80
Disabled American Veterans, 130
Disabled American Veterans'
  Memorial, 130. See also Angel Fire

Distinguished Flying Cross, 109
Dog Soldiers, 33
Doy, John, 29

Ellis, Alice, 11–12
Evans, John, 32–33, 37

54th Massachusetts Colored Infantry, 20
52nd Ohio Infantry, 16
First Colorado Regiment, 30
Fisher, John, 93–96
Fisher, Lavinia, 93–96
Four Great Rivers, 7–8
From Slavery to Affluence: Memories of Robert Anderson, Ex Slave, 124

Georgia Peace Society, 89
German, John, 6
Grant, Ulysses S., 38, 46

Hall, Benjamin, 31
Hamilton, Alexander, 39, 43
Hamilton Light, 39, 43
Harding, Warren G., 47, 50
Harper's Ferry, 29
Harrison, Benjamin, 50, 51
Harrison, William Henry, 50
Hirohito, Emperor of Japan, 73
Hoover, Herbert, 48, 81

Internment camps, 79, 83–84

Japanese Americans. *See* Internment camps
Jackson, Andrew, 51
Jefferson, Thomas, 39, 52
Johnson, Andrew, 17, 38, 50
Johnson, Ed, 80
Johnson, Lyndon B., 50
Johnson, Richard Mentor, 50
Joseph, Chief of Nez Perce, 85, 89

Keith, Daniel, 9–14
Kennedy, John F., 49, 50, 90
Korean War, 103–109

Lakota. *See* Sioux

Lee, Robert E., 38
Lincoln, Abraham, 38
Little Big Horn, 19, 46

"Machine Gun Kelly." *See* Barnes, Bruce Jr.
MacArthur, Arthur, 19
MacArthur, Douglas (General), 19, 62, 63, 64, 82
"Manassa Mauler." *See* Dempsey, William Harrison (Jack)
Marshall, Thomas Riley, 49
Marti, Jóse, 111–120
McKinley, William, 18, 47, 50
Medicine Calf, 4
Medicine Water, 1, 6, 7, 8
Miles, Nelson (Colonel), 6
Miller, Doris, 53–54
Mishima, Yukio, 72
Mochi, 1–8
Moke Tavato (Black Kettle), 2, 4, 5, 6, 32, 33
Morgan, Robert, 97
Mother Maggard, 26–27

Nader, Ralph, 92
National American Woman Suffrage Association, 88
National Consumers League, 89
National Council for the Prevention of War, 90
National Organization of Women, 91
National Vietnam Memorial, 126, 129
Native American tribes. *See* individual tribes: Acoma, Arapaho, Cherokee, Cheyenne, Nez Perce, Sioux, Utes
Native Americans
   Antonio, Sam, 59–70
   Medicine Calf, 4
   Medicine Water, 1, 6, 7, 8
   Mochi, 1–8
   Moke Tavato, 2, 4, 5, 6, 32, 33
   Preston, Billie, 56–58
   Standing Bull, 3
Navy Cross, 54
Nez Perce, 85
Nineteenth Amendment, 88–89

Nixon, Richard, 49
Nobel Peace Prize, 47

125th United States Colored Troops,
   123
Onoda, Hiroo, 73

Pawnee, 6
Pearl Harbor, 53, 55, 62, 78, 80, 82,
   83, 90
Peeples, John, 94–96
Perot, Ross, 20
Pershing, John J. (General), 47
Pirates, 41, 42, 97–101
Preston, Billie, 56–58
Price, George (Captain), 35, 36, 37
Prohibition, 48

Rackham, Jack, 98, 99
Rankin, Jeannette Pickering, 78,
   85–92
Read, Mary, 98–99
Reagan, Ronald, 21
Relocation Act, 78. *See also*
   Internment camps
Rocky Mountain News, 30, 79
Roosevelt, Franklin Delano, 64, 78,
   82, 90
Roosevelt, Theodore, 20, 50
Roosevelt, Theodore Jr., 20

Sand Creek. *See* Sand Creek Massacre
Sand Creek Massacre, 1, 5, 28, 30, 31,
   32, 34, 35, 37
7th Cavalry, 19
Silver, France "Frankie," 96
Simpson, Alan, 20
Sioux, 31, 37
Smith, John, 32
Soule, Silas, 28–38
Spanish American War, 20, 118
Standing Bull, 3
Stockdale, James (Admiral), 20–21
Stowe, Harriet Beecher, 29
Stratemeyer, George (General), 109
Suffrage movement. *See* Women's
   rights

Surrate, Mary, 93

Taft, William Howard, 49, 50
Tappan, Colonel Samuel, 31, 34
Teach, Edward (Blackbeard), 41,
   97–98, 100
Thompson, George H.(General), 16
"Trail of Tears," 51, 56, 57

"Underground railroad," 29
Union Army. *See* Civil War
Utes, 127

Van Buren, Martin, 50
Vietnam Memorial at Angel Fire. *See*
   Angel Fire
Vietnam Memorial in Washington,
   D.C. *See* National Vietnam
   Memorial
Vietnam War, 20–21, 90–91, 126,
   128–131

Wainwright, Jonathan (General), 64,
   65
Walker, Mary Edwards, 15–19
Walker, N. E., 11–14
War of 1812, 40
Washington Equal Suffrage
   Association, 87
Westphall, Victor, 126–131
White Antelope, 2, 33
Wilson, Woodrow, 49
Woman's Peace Party, 88
Women's International League for
   Peace and Freedom, 89
Women's rights, 17, 19, 87–89
Works for Women's Peace Union,
   89
World War I, 20, 88, 89
World War II, 20, 53, 59, 62–70, 71,
   78–82, 90
Wounded Knee, South Dakota, 19
Wynkoop, Edward (Major), 30, 31, 32,
   35

Yokoi, Shoichi, 71–73
York, Alvin C. (Corporal), 20

CPSIA information can be obtained at www.ICGtesting.com
Printed in the USA
LVOW06s2202100815

449632LV00013B/254/P